1595   10.00
        ce

Pottersfield Press

CRIME WAVE

*Con Men, Rogues and Scoundrels
from Nova Scotia's Past*

DEAN JOBB

Pottersfield Press, Lawrencetown Beach,
Nova Scotia, Canada, 1991

Canadian Cataloguing in Publication Data

Jobb, Dean, 1958-

Crime Wave

ISBN 0-919001-68-8

1. Crime -- Nova Scotia --History. 2. Criminals -- Nova Scotia --History. I. Title.

HV6809.N6J62 1991   364.9716   C91-097611-2

Published with the assistance of The Nova Scotia Department of Tourism and Culture and The Canada Council

Pottersfield Press
Lawrencetown Beach
RR 2, Porters Lake
Nova Scotia B0J 2S0

Printed in Canada

To the memory of my father,
Wendell Leon Jobb.

CONTENTS

Frederick Henry More. Henry J. Moon. William Newman. Henry More Smith. By whatever alias, he was one
of the most brazen thieves and con-men to ply his trade
in the Maritimes.

When P.T Barnum's famous circus came to Halifax for the
first time in the summer of 1876, a couple of enterprising
robbers helped prove his maxim: "There's a sucker born
every minute."

Rich, cultured and a bit of a ladies' man, the affable Lou
Keytes cut a swath through Halifax social circles in 1924.
There was just one problem—the Chicago authorities
had a few questions about the millions he had bilked out
of investors under his real name, Leo Koretz.

Samuel Herbert Dougal made headlines in 1903 when he
was hanged for killing his lover and plundering her fortune. A quarter of a century earlier, Dougal had two
wives die in Halifax within four months. Was it coincidence, or was Dougal an old hand at murder?

After the explosion of 1917 devastated Halifax, the hunt
was on for scapegoats. The captain and pilot of the
French munitions ship *Mont Blanc* survived the blast,
only to find themselves charged with manslaughter.

Fire swept through Halifax's venerable Queen Hotel on
a bitterly cold morning in 1939, killing twenty-eight
people. If the hotel's owner had installed proper safety
equipment, could more lives have been saved?

Introduction

Crime always seems impossible in retrospect.
Stephen Leacock

On a hot summer day in 1876, a daring robber with an impeccable sense of timing pulled a bank job in Halifax that, looking back, sounds more like fiction than fact. He accomplished the feat in broad daylight, and while the sidewalk in front of the main branch of the Bank of Nova Scotia was packed with hundreds of people waiting for a circus parade to pass. After the clerks closed their wickets, locked the front door, and ducked outside to catch a glimpse of the wonders of the Big Top, he slipped in a side door, made an unscheduled withdrawal of $22,000, and fled.

Sound impossible? There's more. Mild-mannered, bespectacled Leo Koretz talked hundreds of people into buying stocks in a bogus Panamanian oil syndicate; he was so convincing, his victims even joked that he was taking them to the cleaners. Henry More Smith was a versatile criminal who feigned sickness to escape jail cells and insanity to escape the gallows. Teenager James Bowie gunned down his neighbour under the nose of the local constable and made a clean getaway. And the crude but charming Samuel Herbert Dougal managed to dispose of two wives within four months without arousing the slightest suspicion.

Koretz, Dougal, Smith and Bowie are not household names, but they are as much a part of Nova Scotia's past as Joseph Howe and Charles Tupper. More infamous than famous, they have earned a place in history thanks not to their good deeds, but through their misdeeds. This book is a collection of thirteen stories of crimes and criminals—some serious, some offbeat—drawn from two centuries of Nova Scotia history.

Confidence men, pirates, murderers, pimps—they're all here. But not all the people you are about to meet were hardened criminals. George Preeper, for one, was simply in the wrong place at the wrong time. For Preeper, that meant an encounter with a mob bent on deciding an election with sticks, stones and fists. John Simon, on the other hand, found himself in legal hot water for something he neglected to do—preventing his seedy hotel from becoming a fire trap. And the unfortunate officers of the munitions ship *Mont Blanc* were convenient targets for the wrath of a city devastated by the biggest non-nuclear explosion in history.

All these stories have Nova Scotia as a backdrop, but few of the central characters are Bluenosers. Nova Scotia has had the dubious honour of playing host to a motley collection of criminals from around the world. Dougal and Smith dropped in from England to commit murder and theft. When the heat was on in Chicago, Koretz thought the province's backwoods was the prefect place to live on the lam in style. In the last century, a succession of pirates and mutineers washed up on Nova Scotia's shores for trial and execution.

While the stars of the show are often newcomers, there is a strong local supporting cast. James W. Johnston, William Young, Brenton Halliburton, and William Blowers Bliss were the most prominent legal figures of their time, and they crop up in more than one of these stories as lawyers, judges, or both. But Horace A. Flemming would barely rate a footnote in any book except for an incredible coincidence. In 1876, as a 19-year-old bank clerk, he barely kept his job after the Bank of Nova Scotia was robbed during the circus parade; half a century later, after a distinguished career with the bank, he helped nab Leo Koretz, swindler extraordinaire.

These stories have previously appeared in *The Novascotian*, a weekly supplement to *The Chronicle-Herald* and *The Mail-Star*. I am grateful to the newspapers' managing editor, Jane Purves, for granting permission to reproduce photographs, cartoons and advertisements from the *Herald*'s files. A succession of editors at the helm of *The Novascotian*—Bill March, Lorna Inness, Claire McIlveen—have encouraged me to keep digging into Nova Scotia's legal past.

Staff at the Public Archives of Nova Scotia, the Legislative Library, the National Archives of Canada and the Nova Scotia Barristers Society Library handled numerous requests for material. Alberta Dubé, the *Herald*'s librarian, was constantly called on to help find files and illustrations. Peter Parsons and Mike Harvey of Clark Photographic tracked down and reproduced many of the photographs that accompany these stories.

Pat Duncan continues to be an unerring source of insights into how the justice system works, or should work. Pam Sword proofread the manuscript, and suggested the quote to lead off the introduction. Bruce Erskine gave the page proofs a final check. And Lesley Choyce, who made my day by seeking out this book, jump-started the project with a dose of his infectious enthusiasm.

Dean Jobb
Halifax, Nova Scotia, June 1991

Part One

A fool and his money

Chapter 1

The mysterious stranger

During the summer of 1812, Haligonians found themselves under attack. War had just broken out between Britain and the United States, but Halifax was under siege by a different enemy. The homes of wealthy residents were stripped of fine silver and other valuables in the night; shops and offices were looted. No one was immune to the crime wave. Even the colony's chief justice, Sampson Salter Blowers, had three admiralty law books swiped from his chambers.

The chief justice promptly offered a reward of three pounds for the return of the missing volumes, no questions asked. Within days, a Windsor man named Henry More Smith came forward and claimed the reward. Although Smith swore he had bought the books from a stranger, he became the prime suspect in the rash of thefts.

At first glance, he seemed an unlikely candidate for the role of burglar. A well-dressed, polite man in his mid-twenties, Smith had arrived in Windsor earlier that year looking for work. He said he was a tailor by trade, and had recently emigrated from England. "He was perfectly inoffensive, gentle and obliging," by one account, "used no intoxicating liquors, refrained from idle conversation and all improper language and was apparently free from every evil habit."

Little was known about Smith's past. He told people he was a native of Brighton, England, and had lived briefly in the United States. He once made the dubious claim that he was Cambridge educated, could speak five languages and had five hundred pounds in the Bank of England. One thing was certain: he had received some religious instruction. Smith usually toted a Bible, could recite whole chapters of Scripture, and professed to have conducted Methodist prayer meetings in England.

Smith's apparent religious devotion impressed John Bond, who hired Smith to work on his farm in Rawdon, a few miles east of Windsor. Bond, a strict Baptist, was pleased to see his hired man faithfully attend the family's morning and evening prayers. When Bond was absent, Smith officiated. Besides winning his employer's trust, he won the heart of Bond's daughter, Elizabeth. They were married in Windsor on March 12, 1813. Smith went into business for himself as a tailor and pedlar.

But it was not long before the locals began to observe something strange about the newcomer's behaviour. Smith travelled to Halifax often, always leaving early in the day and returning the next morning. He invariably brought back a variety of articles and, after one trip, a large sum of money.

Suspicions raised when Smith returned the chief justice's law books were soon confirmed. A man nabbed on a Halifax street while wearing a stolen coat protested that he had purchased the garment from a Windsor tailor named Smith. The authorities issued a warrant for Smith's arrest, but by the time word reached Rawdon, Smith had abandoned his wife and fled.

It was the beginning of long criminal career for Henry More Smith, the most brazen and proficient con man, horse thief, burglar, escape artist and all-around rogue ever to ply his nefarious trade in the Maritime provinces. He cut a swath of crime across Nova Scotia and New Brunswick, stealing horses, silverware, clothing, pocket watches—anything of value he could lay his hands on. Along the way he went under a string of aliases: Smith, Frederick Henry More, Henry J. Moon, William Newman.

After making his getaway from Windsor, Smith disappeared for almost two years. He surfaced in July 1814, entering Saint John, New Brunswick, on foot. Once in the city he fell in with a Colonel Daniel of the Ninety-ninth Regiment. Noticing the officer's carriage team did not match, Smith said he had seen the mate to the colonel's black horse just over the border in Nova Scotia. A deal was struck. For fifty pounds, Smith would return to Nova Scotia and buy the horse for the colonel. Pocketing a fifteen pound advance, Smith was off.

He may have intended to fulfil the agreement with the colonel, but not by legitimate means. His first stop was in Norton parish, about thirty miles to the east. There, on July 20, Smith stole a horse belonging to Wills Frederick Knox and headed to Nova Scotia. Smith picked the wrong horse. Knox, son of a British undersecretary of state, was a local magistrate, gentleman farmer, and relentless defender of his property. Discovering the theft the following afternoon, Knox formed a posse of one and gave chase. Four days later, thanks to information from residents who had seen a stranger pass, Knox caught up to Smith in Pictou, some 280 miles away. Smith was arrested and, after several escape attempts, was brought back to Kingston, New Brunswick, to await trial.

While imprisoned in Kingston, Smith met the man who would cash in on his villainy by chronicling his life. Walter Bates, the fifty-four-year-old Kings County sheriff, became obsessed with his prisoner, hanging on his every word and embellishing many of his exploits. He confessed he saw in Smith "a character singular and unprecedented." Bates immortalized Smith in a rambling book entitled *The Mysterious Stranger or Memoirs of the Noted Henry More Smith*. First published in Connecticut, the book reached a wide audience in the Maritimes—a Halifax newspaper, *The Acadian Recorder*, for instance, serialized it in 1817 and sold copies for a shilling. The book was a commercial success, running to seven printings. The last appeared in 1912, the centenary of Smith's arrival in Nova Scotia.

But, for the time being, Bates had his hands full keeping Smith inside the walls of a twenty-two by sixteen foot cell. As September 27, the date for trial, approached, Smith complained of a severe pain in his side—the result, he said, of Knox striking him with a pistol butt. His condition worsened steadily and doctors were called in, but medicine failed to slow his decline. On September 24, barely able to raise his head, Smith dictated his will. "I fear we shall be disappointed in our expectations of the trial of the prisoner, More Smith, at the approaching court," Bates wrote Smith's defence lawyer, Charles Peters of Saint John. "I presume from his appearance he will be removed by death before that time."

That afternoon, Smith cried out in agony and asked the guard to heat a brick to warm his feet. Unable to deny comfort to a dying man, the guard complied, leaving the cell door open. When he returned a few minutes later, Smith had vanished without a trace. Smith's stellar performance left Sheriff Bates and the jailor looking like fools, but not everyone was laughing. When court convened, the grand jury made up for Smith's absence by returning indictments against both men for negligence in allowing a prisoner to escape.

Meanwhile, a province-wide search was launched and Attorney General Thomas Wetmore posted a reward for Smith's capture. Smith was not hard to track—in his wake he left a trail of plundered houses. Reports began pouring in. Smith stole a silver watch, eight dollars cash and other articles from a home ten miles away, then continued westward, toward the American border, stopping at a tavern for breakfast and swiping a set of silver teaspoons. In Maugerville, he stole a pair of boots; outside Fredericton, he raided a trunk in an inn and made off with expensive clothes. He almost was detected near Woodstock when a fellow passenger in a canoe recognized his silver watch as the one reported stolen. Smith managed to talk his way out of the predicament and continued his flight.

The gift of gab served Smith well. He pretended to be a businessman and told other people he was tracking an army deserter. At one point, he even had the audacity to pose as a searcher hot on the trail of a notorious horse thief who had broken out of Kingston jail. But news of his exploits overtook him before he could reach the United States border, and he was arrested October 10. Smith, his hands and feet in chains, was sent back to Kingston under guard. Despite the security measures, he managed to break free the first night and disappeared into the darkness.

Returning to the Fredericton area, he stole a saddle, bridle and pony. Then he paid an unofficial call on Attorney General Wetmore, who was entertaining at his home near the city. Undetected, Smith entered the front door and made off with a variety of coats guests had left hanging in the hall. Smith was found a few days later, holed up in a barn with the stolen clothing hidden beneath the hay. He was returned to Kingston, where elaborate steps had been taken for his accommodation. He was ordered to strip to his shirt and searched, then chained to the floor by one leg. Neither sheriff nor jailer could risk another embarrassing escape.

The sound of filing was soon heard from the cell. On inspection, guards found Smith had cut his leg chain and was nearly through the bars on the window. Asked for his tools, he readily produced a file and crude saw made from a knife blade. The tools were seized and the chain replaced, but the noise persisted. This time, Smith was told to remove all his clothes; a ten-inch saw blade was found tied tightly inside his thigh by a string. Drastic measures were in order. Bates commissioned a blacksmith to bind Smith in an iron collar and leg fetters, both bolted to the floor with chain to restrict his movements, and attached by chain to a set of handcuffs. The portable prison weighed forty-six pounds.

Smith took a new tack, shouting like a madman and loudly quoting Scripture. He tried to hang himself with his chains and was bound even tighter. The prisoner responded by refusing to speak for days at a time and beating his chains against the cell floor, sometimes managing to break them. He was often found with his wrists and ankles bloody and swollen from attempts to free himself.

Smith's trial on a charge of stealing Knox's horse opened May 4, 1815. In the prisoner's dock he continued to play the role of the lunatic, loudly snapping his fingers and tearing at his shirt. He managed to kick the wooden railing in front of him to pieces before constables could restrain him. Smith's lawyer, Peters, put up a strong defence, based mainly on the premise that possession was not proved because Smith was not found riding the horse in

16

Thief, burglar, escape artist, con man—the versatile Henry More Smith was a one-man crime wave. (New Brunswick Museum)

Pictou. The jury deliberated two hours and found him guilty. The sentence was death by hanging.

Attorney General Wetmore, who conducted the prosecution even though he had been among Smith's victims, ordered a report on the prisoner's conduct before setting a date for execution. Bates went to Smith's cell to explain the seriousness of the situation. "He paid no attention," the sheriff reported, "patted his hands, sang and acted the fool as usual."

Smith had little trouble devising a way to fill his final hours. Using straw from his bedding and his own clothes, he constructed about a dozen puppets he called his "family," and put on shows for the locals. Then he claimed to be able to tell fortunes from tea leaves. In August, after diligent efforts by his lawyer, Smith was pardoned, based on his youth and, no doubt, the strong indications he was insane. Smith played the role to the hilt. When Bates told him the news, he replied: "I wish you would bring me some new potatoes when you come again."

A condition of the pardon was that Smith leave New Brunswick, where other warrants were outstanding for his arrest. Bates, who had grown fond of his prisoner despite the grief he had caused during a year behind bars, gave Smith a new set of clothes and paid his passage on a ship bound for Windsor, a short sail across the Bay of Fundy. Bates assumed Smith would return to his wife, but Smith had other ideas. As soon as the boat docked he dropped the insane act and returned to his the job he knew best—stealing.

Smith headed south and a few years later was arrested for taking jewelry, money, and dozens of silver spoons from an innkeeper in New Haven, Connecticut. After trying the deathbed routine for a second time, he sawed through his cell door but was recaptured. Convicted of burglary at trial, Smith—he now called himself William Newman—was sentenced to three years at hard labour. Bates travelled from New Brunswick and verified it was the same man. Smith, however, acted as if he had never seen Bates before.

After his release, Smith's path begins to fade. Bates claims Smith committed more crimes in Boston, New York, Connecticut and Upper Canada. He also accused Smith of posing as a preacher named Henry Hopkins in one of the southern states before he was arrested sometime before 1827 and sentenced to seven years in prison. But Bates' identification of Smith as the culprit is dubious, based only on reports of the methods used in the crimes. If a criminal showed extraordinary guile, Bates was convinced it was Smith. He failed to consider that there could be other artful horse thieves on the loose. In an era when even petty offences were punishable by death, Smith was not the only one to risk a life of crime.

In 1807, to cite at least one other example preserved in print, an American published an autobiography entitled *A Narrative of the Life, Adventures, Travels and Sufferings of Henry Tufts*. Tufts, like Smith, was a one-man crime wave. In the late 1700s, he travelled the backroads of New England, stealing some fifty horses and posing as everything from a preacher to an Indian medicine man. In 1795 he, too, was sentenced to hang for theft but lived to steal another day. The sentence was commuted to life in prison and, after serving five years, Tufts escaped.

Despite his illegal lifestyle, Smith had some redeeming qualities. "In all the adventures which the history of his course presents to our view," Bates wrote at the end of *The Mysterious Stranger*, "we are not called upon to witness any acts of violence and blood, and it is perhaps owing to the absence of this repulsive trait that we do not behold him in a more relentless light." A cynical Saint John publisher, writing in the preface to the book's fifth edition in 1887, was even more charitable. "Had Smith lived in our day," he mused, "his genius would have earned for him a foremost place in the politics of the country."

TO MY FRIENDS

— IN —

NEW BRUNSWICK AND NOVA SCOTIA.

I AM POSITIVELY COMING,

IN PERSON.

For the First Time to Visit You,

WITH MY NEW AND

GREATEST SHOW ON EARTH!

AND WILL ADDRESS MY PATRONS AT EACH EXHIBITION.

P. T. BARNUM'S

Great Travelling World's Fair!

IN ALL ITS OVERSHADOWING VASTNESS,

IS COMING,

IN THREE MONSTER SPECIAL RAILROAD TRAINS!

AND WILL EXHIBIT AT

HALIFAX,

TUESDAY, WEDNESDAY, and THURSDAY,
August 1st, 2nd, and 3rd.

$1,500,000 Cash Capital Invested!! 1100 Persons and 600 Horses and Ponies employed by it!! A Century's Festival of Features in a Metropolis of Separate Tents!!!

ITS NOAH-LIKE MENAGERIE! Is 100 Per Cent The LARGEST ever moved.

Sixty Cages of Rare Animals and Amphibia,

Advertisements for P.T. Barnum's circus performances in Halifax in the summer of 1876 promised a "Noah-like menagerie" of exotic animals.(*Chronicle-Herald/Mail Star* files)

Chapter 2

Three-ring robbery

I t was billed as "The Greatest Show on Earth," and it was coming to Halifax for the first time. Special trains were arranged to bring thousands of spectators to the Nova Scotia capital on the first three days of August 1876 to see P.T. Barnum's Circus. Advertisements and billboards, using money as a measure of the show's grandeur, boasted the spectacle was worth $1.5 million, paid $2,000 a day in salaries, and filled three "monster" trains.

Patrons were promised "a Noah-like menagerie" of exotic animals, including the only living hippopotamus in North America. Headlining the show's human marvels was Captain Costentenus, a Greek man who had been tattooed from head to foot with 388 pictures of "birds, beasts and men ... for engaging in rebellion against the King." Horsemen, acrobats, trapeze artists, trained elephants, a museum of curiosities and artifacts "from every Clime," and a portrait gallery of "the most distinguished Rulers and Statesmen of the Old and New World" were also featured.

Admission to the entire show, which was crammed into three tents set up on the Halifax Commons, was fifty cents, a quarter for children under nine, and free to those willing to shell out a princely $1.50 for the nine-hundred-page, illustrated Life of P.T. Barnum. Halifax was in the midst of a summer heatwave and turnout was heavy; some 9,000 tickets were sold for one of the evening performances in a city of 30,000. "There may not be much money in Halifax," noted The Morning Herald, "but there will no doubt be enough found to enable every man and his neighbor to be there at some time during the show's stay."

There was no shortage of money at the Bank of Nova Scotia on Hollis Street, a two-storey stone building replete with pillars and gargoyles located one door north of George Street. And even bank clerks found it hard to resist the lure of the Big Top. On Wednesday morning, August 1, Barnum's performers staged a massive promotional parade down Hollis Street, the heart of city's mercantile and financial district. As it passed the front doors of the bank about half past eleven, employees abandoned their desks and wickets and joined the throngs of spectators on the sidewalk.

"There was nothing said about going out to see the show among any of the clerks," recalled St. George Twining, who had been a teller at the bank for almost four years. "The movement towards the door was general." All eight employees, including John Nalder, an accountant who was in charge while the cashier was out of town, grabbed their hats and headed outside.

Nalder instructed one of the tellers to lock the door. In his haste to catch a glimpse of the parade, he did not stop to make sure the order was carried out. But Horace Flemming, one of the clerks, locked the door and gave it a rattle to make sure it was secure. They were out of the building ten minutes, fifteen tops. Melville Whidden was the first to return. "I found no one there," he swore. "I unlocked the door myself, no one was inside."

Twining returned to work at his desk. It was another fifteen minutes before he reached for the cashbox he kept in an unlocked drawer. To Twining's shock, it was empty. When he had received it from the safe earlier that morning, it had been stuffed with roughly $17,000 in small bills. More than half was in Bank of Nova Scotia twenty-dollar notes, but there were also bundles of Canadian and Newfoundland currency.

"I first spoke to Mr. Nalder and asked him if he had been meddling with my money," Twining said, thinking he was being made the butt of a joke. He also accused Flemming of hiding the cash. But Flemming, he discovered, was trying to find about $5,000 that had been in his own desk before the parade passed. It was no joke. Twining sheepishly entered the office of the bank's president, who had just arrived at work, to break the news: Somehow, someone had cleaned out the till to the tune of $22,000.

Word reached the Halifax police station, just a block away at the corner of George Street and Bedford Row, about noon. Sergeants Nicholas Power and Daniel McDonald were dispatched to investigate. Power, a burly Royal Navy veteran who had been with the force for a dozen years, took charge and began interviewing witnesses. The only lead came from Mary Anderson, the wife of one of the bank's messengers, who lived upstairs. About the time the circus parade passed, she said, there was a ring at the side door, a private entrance serving the upstairs apartments. She answered the door and was confronted by a stranger who said he had dropped a "valuable paper" down the sidewalk grate. He wanted to go to the basement to try to retrieve it.

There was nothing strange about the request. Anderson was used to fetching items lost down the grate, but the man pushed past her and said he would get it himself. "Which way?" he asked as he hurried down the hall. "Down there," Anderson replied, surprised by the man's boldness. He disappeared into the cellar.

Anderson stood at the door and stared down the hall as she waited for the visitor to return. After about four minutes, he rushed past her from the other direction. He had taken a second stairway leading from the cellar to the bank, then cut through the bank's boardroom to return to the side door. Anderson was again taken by surprise. "He stepped past me so quick that I just asked him if he got the paper; he said 'Yes,' and began to run." He headed south on Hollis Street and disappeared into the crowds. Anderson, who had no idea the bank was empty, thought nothing more of the encounter until the clerks discovered they had been robbed.

The policemen were able to extract only the barest description of the man: short, wore dark clothes and a hat, walked with a gait. It wasn't much to go on, but Power suspected whoever had pulled off the daring heist would be trying to make a getaway. He and McDonald headed for the railway station in the north end of the city.

At Flinn's Hotel, near the depot, they hit paydirt. Two men, one answering the description, had dropped in to ask where they could hire a wagon. That tip lead the policemen to William Hinch, a cabman who lived nearby. Yes, Hinch said, two men, one tall and one short, had tried to hire him about half past twelve. He told them the fare would be five dollars. The shorter man reached into his pocket and pulled out a wad of bills "nearly as thick as my wrist," Hinch said, and peeled off some tens and twenties. He asked his companion if he had a five, and the tall man produced a smaller bundle of bills and found a five.

"I asked them to wait til I got a bite of dinner," Hinch told the policemen. "They said no, they were in a great hurry, they wanted to meet some friends in Bedford." Hinch lined them up with another driver and the pair left. Each man carried a suitcase and the taller one had a small leather satchel tucked under his arm. Large bundles of bills, suitcases, a short man in a hurry to leave town—Power and McDonald were convinced they were on the right trail.

Hinch had passed the business on to a fellow driver, Jonathan Adams. The two men asked to stop at Four Mile House, an inn on the road to Bedford, and invited Adams in for a beer. The shorter man bought the round. They said they were "circus men," and Adams noted that they left all three pieces of luggage outside in the wagon while they drank. He left his passengers at the Bedford railway station about two-thirty and returned to Halifax.

Stationmaster George Boggs looked up from his newspaper. To his disgust, two men were sitting in the waiting room reserved for women, one puffing on a cigar. "Gentlemen," he growled after opening his office window, "are you aware you are in the ladies room? Furthermore, you are smoking, which is not allowed."

"Really," said the shorter man. "We'll attend to that." Boggs returned to his desk and resumed reading, but looked up a few minutes later to see the two men were still there. "When I speak, I expect to be minded ... you will be good enough to walk out." They went outside, but re-entered on the gentlemen's side of the station, rapped on Boggs's window and asked when the next train would be through from Halifax. The Truro freight was due in at four o'clock, the Pictou Express at 5:05, he told them. Either train would take them where they said they were headed: Windsor Junction. They lingered on the platform for a few minutes, then walked over to French's Hotel.

They were sitting down to their meal in the hotel's dining room when Power and McDonald walked in. There was no one else in the room. "I immediately noticed the short man answered the description given me, and immediately arrested them," Power recalled. "I told them it was for the Bank robbery. They said it was all right or something to that effect."

The men refused to give their names or answer any questions. Power searched the shorter man and found a loaded revolver in his pants pocket. He also had twenty dollars in U.S. greenbacks and three dollars in Canadian currency. McDonald searched the other man and found a watch and no more than thirty-five dollars in American bills. There were no thick wads of money like the cabman Hinch had seen. Power retrieved two valises from a room the pair had rented; they contained clothing and a black felt hat.

While Power was out of the room, the short man turned to McDonald and asked: "Were there any more arrested for the affair?"

"What affair?" the policeman asked.

"You must know."

It was a brief exchange, but it implied others were involved. Power already suspected as much, and continued on to Truro while McDonald escorted the suspects back to Halifax. Under questioning, the short man said he was C.T. Watson from New York. The taller man gave the name Charles G. Hampton of Springfield, Massachusetts.

That night, Anderson was brought to the police station. She could not identify Watson as the man who entered the bank. But he was wearing a black and white straw hat and a light-coloured overcoat. Next morning she was brought back to take another look. This time Power, who was back from Truro, put the black felt hat from one of the valises on Watson's head. "I would not take an oath positively," she said, "but to the best of my belief that is the man."

The identification was shaky, but it was bolstered by Anderson's servant. Before the circus procession passed the bank, Elizabeth Langille went to the side door to take a delivery from the bakery. Just outside, a short man dressed in a dark coat and felt hat was casually leaning against the building. "Has the show gone by?" she asked the man.

"No, not for an hour," he replied.

Shown Watson at the police station, Langille said she had "no doubt" he was the man. Watson and Hampton were charged with robbery and locked up to await a court hearing.

The bank clerks were chastised for displaying "the careless-ness of children and and curiosity of nursery maids" when news of the robbery broke on August 2. "That grown men, with average intellects, should abandon the care of large sums of money, and leave their desks unlocked, to go out to gaze like raw bumpkins at a passing show," fumed *The Morning Herald*, "is something that excites one's scorn too much to leave room for any pity for the victims of the clever rascality which followed."

But the Bank of Nova Scotia's employees were not the only ones who were red-faced. Less than a block away, in the treasury office at Province House, a cash box containing about $2,000 had been swiped after a similar rush to see the parade. The box was later found on a nearby wharf, stripped of everything but two dollars in change. The bank offered a $2,000 reward for the conviction of the robbers; the government put up five hundred dollars for its assailant.

The *Herald* felt The Greatest Show on Earth was partly to blame. "There is no doubt that the circus was followed by some desperate ruffians, and the city is well rid of them," the paper editorialized on August 5. "Thieves hang around Barnum like the cloud of camp followers around an Indian army." It was a harsh assessment, but truth was the circus tended to leave empty tills in its wake. The day before the show came to Halifax, the train station in Truro was robbed of one hundred dollars while the circus was performing in the town.

There were strong indications Watson and Hampton were among those cashing in on the pandemonium created by Barnum's show. Hampton, described as "a noted New York thief" in the press, had served time for robbery in the United States and went by the alias Horace Hampton. Both men refused to pose for photographs that would help police confirm their identities. Officers hauled them to a commercial studio, but by one report, "they fought and struggled and 'pulled faces'" and ruined every print. Watson later explained their lack of co-operation by alleging that police had "abused and beaten" them.

Police were also searching for at least one other suspect. Neither man had the loot when arrested, and the small leather satchel they had when dropped off in Bedford was missing when they were arrested a little more than an hour later. Had it been passed to an accomplice? Hampton told police he had taken a room at the International Hotel the night before the robbery. A porter said he had seen Watson, Hampton and a third man outside the hotel shortly before the robbery. Further inquiries showed Hampton and a W.H. DeWitt had signed for the room, and Hampton had left a message for a B. Johnston. But those names led nowhere. A week after the robbery, a Halifax detective went to New York to question a man who had been arrested for trying to pass four hundred dollars in Bank of Nova Scotia notes. But no charges were laid and the man was released.

There was also talk that the robbery had been in inside job. At least one city newspaper put those rumours into print, drawing a stern rebuke from the *Herald*. "Rumours, affecting the *honesty* of the bank officials, and hints of collusion, are baseless, and are very unkind to those who are already suffering deeply from the consequences of their neglect." The *Herald*, which had been quick to scold the clerks, now leapt to their defence. "The young men yielded to an impulse to which nine tenths of the population able to walk would have yielded," the paper noted on August 5. "The Bank clerks only did as other mortals did."

But the whole scam reeked of collusion. If Watson had swiped the cash, how did he know he could get inside the bank through the cellar? The robber had to duck in, rifle the desks, pocket the money and duck out, all in less than five minutes. Somehow, the robber had made a beeline for the desks of the only tellers who had large sums of money. It was as if he knew the safe and cashier's room, both containing large amounts of money, were locked. And how could the man seen waiting by the side door have known the bank would be empty, and for how long? The timing was too perfect.

But Bank of Nova Scotia officials had little interest in answering those questions. The directors huddled in an emergency session within hours of the robbery, but there was no internal investigation and no search of the premises for the money. Perhaps the directors wanted to leave well enough alone. Only six years earlier, an audit had revealed that James Forman, chief cashier since the bank was founded in 1832, had embezzeled more than $300,000—in those days, roughly half the bank's capital. That scandal had been kept under wraps, and no one was eager to uncover a new one.

That did not stop heads from rolling. St. George Twining, who had lost the bulk of the cash, was fired for carelessness about a month after the robbery. The other teller who was stung, Horace Flemming, was fired but later rehired. Nalder, the accountant who was in charge on the day of the robbery, was also fired. Within days of the robbery he announced he had received an urgent telegram from his father and had to return to England. He left on the next steamer. Nalder's hasty departure added fuel to the rumours of collusion.

While the bank employees were facing the music, Watson and Hampton were ordered to stand trial in Supreme Court. Offered a chance to make a statement at the close of a drawn-out preliminary hearing, both men proclaimed their innocence. Watson showed an astonishing grasp of British law by citing legal texts to dispute the magistrate's finding that a trial was warranted; Hampton merely protested he was "dangerously ill." Trial was set for November.

The main branch of the Bank of Nova Scotia in Halifax was the target of a daring daylight robbery. (*Chronicle-Herald/Mail-Star* files)

From that point on, the case took on the appearances of a circus that would rival Barnum's. First, a prosecutor had to be found. The attorney general personally handled Halifax criminal cases, but Otto Weeks, who had held the post for about a year, rarely appeared in court and was neglecting his departmental duties. His problem was the bottle, and it became so acute that Premier P.C. Hill was forced to remove him from office in late November 1876.

Weeks's absences forced the government to hire lawyers to handle prosecutions. James McDonald, a Pictou Scot with twenty-five years at the bar and a reputation as one of the finest courtroom lawyers of the day, had handled the preliminary hearing for Watson and Hampton. On November 1, Premier Hill asked Samuel Leonard Shannon to prosecute that month's criminal cases before the Supreme Court. Shannon, sixty, was the senior Queen's Counsel in Halifax, but in his thirty-seven years of practice he had specialized in real estate and wills, not criminal law. "In the case of the Bank robbery," the premier noted in a letter to Shannon, "as Mr. McDonald attended to the preliminary investigations, he had better take charge of the indictment." Shannon did most of the talking at trial, but took his cues from McDonald.

Watson and Hampton, meanwhile, had retained the cream of the Halifax defence bar—Robert Motton, whose busy criminal practice kept his name in the papers virtually every day; Robert Weatherbe, talented but quick-tempered, a future chief justice of Nova Scotia; and R.G. Haliburton, son of judge and humorist Thomas Chandler Haliburton.

The defence strategy as the evidence unfolded was simple: throw suspicion on the clerks. Each Bank of Nova Scotia employee who testified was asked point-blank if he knew who had taken the money. Much was made of the accountant's departure for England in the wake of the robbery. And the defence even dredged up the fact that the tellers had come up four hundred dollars short on an earlier occasion.

Those tactics drew the wrath of the *Herald*. On November 25, beside an account of the day's evidence, the paper published a brief editorial: "We would be sorry to interfere in cases under the consideration of the court, but we cannot forbear saying that any attempt by the defence to throw the blame of the robbery of the Bank of Nova Scotia on any of the clerks of that institution, will be visited by the indignation of the whole community."

In court later that day, Weatherbe contended the item had been "maliciously inserted for the purpose of creating a prejudice against the prisoners and depriving them of a fair trial." He went further, alleging that Shannon, a shareholder in the newspaper, had the item inserted to aid the prosecution's case. Shannon, however, assured the court the statements had been published "without my knowledge or consent."

In the course of the debate, a junior lawyer for the prosecution made a crack about a paragraph on the same page that termed Weatherbe the "'Corny Delany' of Barristers." Weatherbe saw red. He denounced the lawyer and the newspaper in such "outrageous language" that the judge issued a stern rebuke and ordered Weatherbe to apologize, to the applause of the spectators. At least that's how the *Herald*, hardly an objective source, described the incident. Undaunted, the defence sought to have Shannon and the *Herald*'s editor found in contempt of court.

Besides scoring points with the bank clerks, the defence hammered away on the identification of Watson as the man who had entered the bank. After extensive questioning by defence lawyers, Anderson and her servant said they could not swear positively that he was the man. After nine days of evidence and legal wrangling, the jury retired at three o'clock on the afternoon of December 2. At nine, the foreman announced that the jurors were deadlocked. According to press reports an initial straw vote had been ten for acquittal, two for conviction; those positions remained unchanged through six hours of deliberation. In the wake of the verdict the motion for contempt was abandoned. The *Herald*'s criticisms had obviously carried little weight with the jurors.

The defence lawyers applied to have Watson and Hampton released pending a retrial. Several prominent doctors submitted letters certifying that Hampton was suffering from lung problems and should be freed; "prolonged [confinement] may perhaps prove fatal," one wrote. Hampton was eventually released on bail and allowed to return to the States; he did not return for the second trial.

Watson was not so lucky. He remained behind bars in Halifax and was tried again in May 1877. By then the press had lost interest in the case. The *Herald*, which published verbatim accounts of the first trial, almost ignored the sequel. This time the jury retired for three hours and returned a verdict of not guilty. The finding prompted "uproarious applause" from the public galleries, claimed one report, and an elated Watson shook hands with the jurors as they filed out. Watson, free for the first time in nine months, celebrated with dinner at a downtown restaurant and caught a train for the States the following night.

No one was ever convicted of the robbery, and the Bank of Nova Scotia never recovered its money. According to a history of the bank published at the turn of the century, Watson went on to serve time for other thefts and once admitted to a detective that he and Hampton had carried out the Halifax heist. If that report is true, the two men made off with $22,000 from a bank in broad daylight when the streets were crammed with people. It was a feat of daring that would have impressed P.T. Barnum himself.

Chapter 3

A swindler with style

L ou Keytes was a ladies' man, and in Nova Scotia at the height of the roaring twenties, there were few more eligible bachelors. Not because of his looks, mind you. A bearded, balding forty-three-year-old, Keytes had stooped shoulders, a distinct paunch and a pasty complexion. Besides, he suffered from severe headaches, and could see little unless he was peering through a pair of thick, wire-rim glasses.

But two things made Keytes the darling of the Halifax social scene in 1924: he had class and, most importantly, he was rich. Filthy rich. Just where he had made his fortune was unclear. Keytes gave few details, telling the curious he had made a killing in real estate in the southern states and had retired to Nova Scotia for his health.

If the source of his money was obscure, there was no doubt he had plenty. After his arrival in Nova Scotia in March 1924, Keytes paid $17,500 cash for a secluded hunting lodge. Called Pinehurst, it was located on two hundred acres in lake-dotted southwestern Nova Scotia, near present-day Kejimkujik National Park. He immediately spent $30,000 to renovate the six-bedroom lodge, furnish it with antiques and install the latest in electrical conveniences. Keytes bought a motor launch to fill the lodge's boathouse, hired a skipper to drive it, and built tennis courts and a croquet lawn on the grounds.

Keytes's spending sprees were legendary. A car dealer in Liverpool, the nearest town, accustomed to buyers paying in instalments, was shocked when Keytes walked in and wrote an

$850 cheque for a new Chevrolet. According to another story, Keytes once bought ice cream at a store in the same town, tendered an American one-hundred-dollar bill, and left without asking for change. It was extravagant spending in the days when a new pair of men's leather shoes sold for three dollars and a woman's fur-trimmed wool winter coat could be picked up on sale at Simpson's department store for $13.95.

Keytes was a lavish entertainer to boot. He threw frequent parties at Pinehurst, sometimes hiring cars to ferry guests to and from the estate. For one soirée, he imported members of the Boston Symphony Orchestra to provide the evening's entertainment. Another party drew one hundred guests, including local businessmen and politicians.

Every fortnight or so, Keytes abandoned his retreat and drove to Halifax to sample the bright lights of the province's capital. "Mr. Keytes was always to be found in the midst of the social swirl in this city," the *Halifax Mail* noted. "Clubs of all sorts, dancing classes, house parties, etc., were ever and anon graced by his presence." He joined the exclusive Royal Nova Scotia Yacht Squadron, was a fixture at the best parties, and hosted dinners at Halifax hotels. He called himself a literary critic, and scoured bookstores for rare books to add to his collection. He was cultured, charming, always immaculately dressed. And it was his taste for fine clothes that proved to be the undoing of the high-flying Lou Keytes.

In early November 1924, eight months after his arrival in the province, Keytes dropped by a Halifax tailor shop, ordered three pairs of silk, fur-trimmed pyjamas worth $150, and left a suit coat for repair. As tailor Francis J. Hiltz worked on the coat, he removed a piece of cloth from the lining. Underneath was the label of the coat's Chicago maker and the name Leo Koretz.

Suspicious, Hiltz took the coat to a prominent banker he knew. Horace Flemming, the sixty-seven-year-old secretary to the board of directors of the Bank of Nova Scotia, checked his records: he could find only one transaction involving Keytes, and it looked legitimate. But Flemming promised to make further inquiries, and sent a telegram to authorities in Chicago on November 19.

Four days later, two policemen walked into a Halifax hotel and arrested Leo Koretz, alias Lou Keytes. Nova Scotia's mysterious socialite was a fugitive wanted in Chicago for bilking scores of investors of at least two million dollars in a Central American oil swindle. After dancing his way into Halifax's social circles, the man described by the city's press as a "social lion" and "a prince of entertainers" was about to face music of another sort.

Relieving the gullible of their money has never been difficult. As Toronto financial writer Diane Francis showed in her book *Contrepreneurs*, fly-by-night promoters have been peddling bogus stocks to the unwary for decades. Today, the scale is international and the proceeds reach into the billions of dollars. In the heady days of the twenties, before the bottom fell out in the Crash of '29, playing the stock market was considered the easy way to wealth and financial security. The steady flow of cash into real estate, oil, mining and other stock promotions offered unlimited opportunities for crooks to line their own pockets.

Witness Boston's Charles Ponzi. Considered the greatest swindler ever to prey on the American public, Ponzi emigrated from his native Italy at the turn of the century. By 1920 he had an offer too good to refuse: fifty percent profit in three months. It worked like this—Ponzi bought international postal-reply coupons in foreign countries at depressed prices and sold them in the United States at a sizeable profit. And, at first, it was legitimate. Then Ponzi began paying dividends not from profits generated, but out of money put up by newer investors. Millions poured in, and the scheme became a giant pyramid; the growing numbers of investors at the bottom of the heap standing little or no chance of getting their money back.

The bubble burst after the *Boston Post* revealed that Ponzi's checkered past included a jail term in Montreal for forgery and a stint behind bars in Atlanta for smuggling illegal aliens. Investment ground to a halt and, without new money to pay interest, the scheme collapsed. Estimates of the amount bilked range from five million to ten million dollars. The *Post* won a Pulitzer for its reporting; Ponzi went to prison for using the mails to defraud and was eventually deported to Italy. He died penniless in South America in 1949.

Koretz proved as adept at the stock swindle as his contemporary. Born in Chicago in 1881, Koretz was the son of middle-class Jewish immigrants from Europe. He grew up speaking German and Bohemian as well as English, and worked as an office boy for a local law firm while studying law. He eventually opened his own practice with what was later described as "indifferent success."

Two incidents helped transform the struggling lawyer into a slick swindler. First, according to his own account, Koretz was part of a group of investors who paid $10,000 for land in Panama. But, when he went south to look at his holdings, he discovered the land was worthless and the seller had never owned it. Then, about 1902, he became involved in a project to transform Arkansas swamp land into rice fields. The plan worked. Koretz made a tidy profit and earned a reputation in Chicago business circles as an astute land speculator.

Somewhere along the line Koretz realized that he could reap more profit from bogus land than from the real thing. Perhaps his own experience at the hands of a con artist had shown him how easily people could be duped. In any event, by 1917 the lawyer-turned-stock promoter was selling shares in a company with an important-sounding name: the Bayano River Timber Syndicate. The firm's location? Why, Panama, of course. The syndicate had supposedly made a fortune selling mahogany cut on its vast landholdings in the Central American country, and was branching out into tropical fruit, grain, ranching, railways, rubber production—you name it. But there was one Bayano product that stood out: oil. Oil to power the cars, airplanes, and ships of an increasingly mechanized world.

Bayano's assets, according to Koretz, were massive: five million acres of land that the syndicate had bought for a dollar an acre; oil wells pumping 250,000 barrels a day; a fleet of a dozen oil tankers. The firm employed 2,500, investors were told, and the Standard Oil conglomerate had offered to pay twenty-five million dollars for a mere one thousand Bayano shares. "When you wish the Bayano a million barrels of oil a month you are a little behind the times," Koretz bragged to Alex Fitzhugh, an Iowa man who bought four hundred shares, "for out of 24 producing wells we are today getting a flush production of about a quarter million barrels per day."

There was no shortage of willing victims. By some accounts, people begged Koretz to invest their money. A dining car steward on the Baltimore & Ohio Railroad handed over his life's savings, $20,000. Investors included Koretz's mother, who put up $50,000, and a brother who shelled out $140,000. Koretz would later claim he had to accept money from his family or risk arousing suspicion.

And, on the surface, Bayano was a money-maker. Shareholders earned a quarterly dividend of five per cent on their investment—a hefty twenty per cent annually. Those dividends, of course, came straight out of new investments as they poured in. It was the Ponzi scheme all over again, but Koretz did the Italian master one better. Instead of paying out cash dividends, he persuaded many investors to pump their paper profits into more worthless Bayano shares.

Koretz enjoyed the good life off Bayano investments, keeping three luxurious offices around Chicago, all well-stocked with booze—shrewdly purchased before prohibition took effect—to quench the thirsts of potential clients. His wife and two children lived in a mansion in the suburbs with terraced gardens overlooking Lake Michigan, and he could even afford to keep a mistress in a South Side apartment.

Faith in Koretz was unshakeable. "Solid business men," one newspaper noted, "came to his office and wrote out their checks and did not even care to take away stocks. They believed in him." After news of Ponzi's fraud broke, some investors, unaware how close they were to the mark, jokingly referred to Koretz as "Lovable Lou ... our Ponzi." On one occasion a group of investors hosted a dinner at a Chicago hotel in honour of their financial wizard. Sitting beside Koretz at the head table was Arthur Brisbane, a top editorial writer for the Hearst newspaper chain and a large investor in Bayano. Suddenly, newsboys burst in with an extra headlined "Leo Koretz oil swindle." There were a few moments of stunned silence before Brisbane told a shaken but relieved Koretz he had had phony papers printed as a practical joke.

But it was not long until real headlines exposed Koretz. In 1922 a half dozen investors proposed to visit Panama to view Bayano's holdings. Koretz managed to stall them for about a year but the group sailed from New York in November 1923. The jig was up, and Koretz meticulously prepared his getaway. He cashed cheques for large sums all over Chicago, stuffing the proceeds into a briefcase and depositing the money each night in the vault of the Drake Hotel.

On December 2, he told relatives assembled for a family dinner that he had sold some of their Bayano stock at an exceptionally good price. He dispersed about $300,000 to his mother, brothers, aunts and in-laws. The next day, he left for New York. Koretz later claimed he took with him only $175,000; the remaining two million dollars that had been sunk into Bayano, he insisted, had been frittered away to pay dividends and to support his lavish lifestyle. He was last seen at the St. Regis Hotel in New York on December 6.

Within days of Koretz's departure, word reached Chicago from the investors touring Panama. There were no oilfields, no tankers, no ranches. In fact, Bayano's lands were owned by the Panamanian government and produced only one commodity—mosquitoes. In February 1924, a grand jury in Chicago indicted Koretz on three counts of using the mails to defraud. That was the tip of the iceberg: more charges of theft, fraud, mail fraud, tax evasion and running a confidence game followed as police and prosecutors dug deeper into the syndicate. The Chicago Title and Trust Company, appointed trustee of Koretz's bankrupt estate, offered a $10,000 reward for his arrest and return to Illinois to face trial. Soon Koretz's pudgy, bespectacled face was staring out from wanted posters in post offices across the United States.

The object of the manhunt was holed up in an apartment on East 48th Street, New York, under the alias Keytes. Koretz grew a beard to mask his identity, and apparently moved freely around America's largest city. In February he bought a New York bookstore for $10,000, helping to establish his new persona as a well-to-do literary critic. Then, by chance, Koretz discovered a possible refuge. Browsing in a sporting goods store, he mentioned to a clerk that he was thinking about buying land in Canada. "There's the man to see," the clerk said, motioning toward another employee. "He's from Nova Scotia."

The employee was L.D. Mitchell, originally from the province's South Shore. He knew just the place—Pinehurst, a rambling lodge that was being sold in the wake of its owner's death. Koretz asked Mitchell to accompany him to Nova Scotia to take a look. Koretz paid the asking price, $17,500, and hired Mitchell as a hunting and fishing guide.

Koretz spared no expense in remodeling Pinehurst into a gentleman's country estate. "All his purchases were paid for in cash and with American bills of large denomination," Mitchell recalled. Despite his benefactor's largesse, Mitchell quit within three months at the urging of his wife, who worked as a housekeeper at the estate. She regarded Koretz as "a peculiar man" and was shocked by the goings on at Pinehurst. Koretz brought home a succession of young women, and at one point shared the premises with a woman from New York and a waitress he had met in Halifax. The New Yorker eventually won the battle for Koretz's affections.

As Koretz built a new life in the backwoods of Nova Scotia, detectives from Chicago tried to pick up his trail. They had one valuable lead: Koretz was a diabetic and needed insulin to survive. Insulin, discovered little more than two years earlier by a Canadian research team lead by Frederick Banting, was still a rare and expensive drug. Investigators doggedly contacted hospitals and doctors in search of an insulin user matching Koretz's description. The trail lead to Canada. In early 1924, police discovered, Koretz had been admitted to a sanatorium in Montreal. From there, he was traced eastward to Nova Scotia.

The law was closing in when, out of the blue, a cable arrived in Chicago from Flemming, the Halifax banker, seeking more information on a man named Leo Koretz. Within days, Patrick McSwiggen of the Chicago Detective Bureau and assistant district attorneys John Sbarbaro and Thomas Marshall descended on Halifax. Enlisting the services of local police, the trap was set for the evening of November 23 at a city hotel where Koretz was staying.

Koretz had just returned to his room after dinner when someone rapped on the door. "What's wanted?" he asked, opening the door to find it flanked by two strangers.

"You are wanted—in Chicago," Halifax Deputy Sheriff R.H. Scriven shot back, grabbing Koretz's wrists as a constable snapped on handcuffs.

"All right boys," Koretz sputtered to his unexpected visitors. "You'll have no trouble from me."

One of the policemen pulled out a wanted poster, and Koretz acknowledged he was the man sought. He was taken to the county jail, where a search of his pockets turned up $450. Questioned by the Chicago contingent that night in his cell, Koretz threw in the towel. He readily admitted his guilt and asked to be returned to Chicago as quickly as possible to face the charges against him. The district attorneys were happy to oblige. "This is the greatest swindle in the history of Cook County," Sbarbaro told reporters, "and people call Chicago the wickedest city in the world."

Spectators lined the halls and staircases of Halifax's ornate, Victorian-era courthouse on Spring Garden Road the next morning to catch a glimpse of the famous swindler, but they were disappointed. Koretz was hustled into Judge W.B. Wallace's office for an arraignment attended only by guards, lawyers and a handful of newsmen.

Koretz looked "pale and worn, as though he had spent a sleepless night," noted one reporter, but "he was still flawlessly dressed" in a green suit and grey, cloth-topped shoes. One thing had changed since the arrest; Koretz was minus the beard he had sported to hide his identity. "It has served its purpose," he had told a barber summoned to his cell earlier in the morning to do the honours. "I want to go back to Chicago clean—like I left there."

After his arrest in Halifax, Leo Koretz, a.k.a. Lou Keytes, posed for photographers outside the Halifax courthouse with his jailor, Malcolm Mitchell. (Public Archives of Nova Scotia/Photograph collection)

Three charges were used to extradite Koretz to the United States, all involving about $38,000 invested in Bayano by a Chicago man, the aptly named Samuel J. Richman. Koretz told the judge he would not fight extradition. The judge ordered him returned to jail for fifteen days—a statutory period to enable an accused to appeal—despite Koretz's offer to waive that right and be taken back to Chicago immediately.

Nova Scotia authorities were wary of Koretz's haste to leave the jurisdiction. The prevailing opinion in local legal circles was that Koretz should fight extradition, if for no other reason than to narrow down the charges against him. Using the mails to defraud, for example, was not an extraditable offence. Attorney General Walter J. O'Hearn ordered the prisoner held until it was established that he had committed no crimes in Nova Scotia. But not only had Koretz paid his way since his arrival, the province had gained by his presence; a cartoon in the *Halifax Herald* depicted Koretz leaving a trail of coins and bills as he headed back to Chicago, under the caption: 'Nova Scotia Loses Another Industry.' Local realtors, car dealers and house renovators were not the only ones to profit from Koretz's sojourn in the province; Hiltz and Flemming, the tailor and banker who had unmasked the fugitive, split the $10,000 reward. And during January 1925, Haligonians lined up for deals when the contents of Pinehurst— furniture, fine linens, sporting goods and the like —were auctioned off at rock-bottom prices.

Back in Chicago, the charges against Koretz were growing daily. Two days after the arrest, Illinois State Attorney Robert E. Crowe announced he would seek three more indictments against Koretz for operating a confidence game. Federal authorities served notice that Koretz faced charges of evading some $750,000 in taxes between 1921 and 1923. But the exact amount defrauded by Koretz has never been determined. Estimates reach as high as five million dollars. According to the authoritative *The Encyclopedia of American Crime*, many businessmen suffered their losses in silence, "fearing that any revelation that they had been swindled would damage their reputations as shrewd businessmen."

The cartoonist for the Halifax Herald took a sardonic view of Koretz's departure and its impact on the Nova Scotia economy. (*Chronicle-Herald/Mail-Star* files)

Koretz was scheduled to leave Halifax by train on the morning of November 29. To accommodate five Chicago reporters who had arrived in Halifax to cover the story, district attorneys Sbarbaro and Marshall arranged a special rail car for the first leg of the trip, to Montreal. The long train ride, it was expected, would enable the newsmen to interview Koretz at length.

While the reporters celebrated their last night in Halifax at a local club, a car swung unseen into the yard behind the county jail. Three men hopped in and the car headed south to Pier Two under cover of darkness. Waiting at the dock were Sbarbaro and Marshall. They and the car's occupants—Koretz, Deputy Sheriff Scriven and Joseph P. Connolly, a young Halifax lawyer acting for Koretz—boarded a steamer that cast off at midnight, bound for New York. Koretz left Nova Scotia as he had arrived—incognito.

On December 3, 1924, exactly one year after he fled Chicago with his loot, Koretz stood before Chief Justice Jacob Hopkins of the Illinois District Court and pleaded guilty to four charges of theft, embezzlement and promoting a confidence game. "Koretz apparently doesn't care," noted one reporter, and he was acting "like a tired man who has resigned himself to his fate." He readily admitted conning scores of people over the better part of a decade.

There was no doubt Koretz would go to prison; the question was for how long. He pleaded guilty to charges that each carried a sentence of one to ten years in prison—a maximum penalty of forty years behind bars. But for Koretz, any prison term would be a life sentence. During the sentencing hearing, a doctor testified that Koretz was seriously ill with diabetes. "Unless there is an immediate improvement, death will probably be the consequence," the court was told. But the chief justice was in no mood to show mercy. He imposed the maximum sentence; under Illinois prison rules, Koretz was looking at a minimum of six years in prison.

That night, a party of armed deputies drove Koretz to the Illinois state prison. Less than two weeks after his arrest in Halifax, prisoner 9463 was stripped of his belongings—fifteen frayed dollar bills, a half-empty can of tobacco, and a box of throat lozenges—and shown to his cell. He was described as "broken in health, shabby in appearance ... cynical and sarcastic in his comment."

Koretz's prison term turned out to be brief. Rather than wait for diabetes to do its job, Koretz decided to take matters into his own hands. On January 6, 1925, little more than a month after he was imprisoned, he convinced a female friend to smuggle in a five-pound box of chocolates. Koretz ate the entire box, lapsed into a coma induced by the massive amount of sugar, and died. It remains one of the most novel prison suicides on record.

Part Two

Deadly business

British soldier Samuel Herbert Dougal was widowed twice within four months while stationed in Halifax. (*Chronicle-Herald/Mail-Star* files)

Fatal attraction

The curt announcements appeared in the Halifax press with startling speed in the summer and early fall of 1885. "Died Lovenia Martha, the wife of Quartermaster Sergeant Samuel Herbert Dougal, Royal Engineers, aged 37 years," the Halifax *Morning Herald* reported on June 29. Six weeks later the same newspaper announced the marriage of Quartermaster Sergeant S.H. Dougal to Mary Herberta Boyd, the daughter of an Irish veterinarian. And then, on October 6, the paper's deaths column noted the passing of Mary Herberta, wife of Quartermaster Sergeant S.H. Dougal. She was only twenty-eight years old and had been a bride a scant two months.

Two wives lost in under four months—this Dougal was a hard luck case, indeed. At least that seems to have been the prevailing opinion. No eyebrows were raised by Dougal's brief period of mourning after his first wife died. If anyone was suspicious after his even younger second wife died just as suddenly, they kept it to themselves.

Another eighteen years would pass before events an ocean away made Dougal's Halifax misfortunes merit a second look. In May 1903 a sensational British murder case grabbed the headlines. The press dubbed it "The Moat Farm Murder," after the remote estate in Essex, northeast of London, where a retired soldier had shot his wealthy mistress to death before plundering her fortune. The accused murderer was a heavy-set, balding man with a demeanor that was purported to be almost as coarse as his flowing beard. His name? Samuel Herbert Dougal. Suddenly the events of 1885 looked less like the product of chance, and more like the result of good management. The British authorities began making inquiries overseas to find out more about Dougal's doings in Halifax.

Dougal ranks as one of the most notorious murderers of Victorian times, an era that had no shortage of villains capable of devising original ways of disposing of unwanted lovers, wives or husbands. Born in London in 1846, Dougal was only nineteen when debts, racked up while living the high life among the low life in the city's bars and music halls, drove him into the military.

A mix of Dr. Jekyll and Mr. Hyde—that's how author F. Tennyson Jesse described Dougal. A keen student of what prompts people to commit murder, she wrote the definitive portrait of Dougal in the late 1920s for the Notable Trials Series— the literary equivalent of the movie-of-the-week treatment sensational crimes receive in our day. As Jekyll, Jesse noted, Dougal emerged from the Royal Engineers after twenty-one years with a spotless service record, a good conduct medal and glowing character references. But Dougal-as-Hyde was a heartless fiend who preyed on women to satisfy his desires and line his pockets. "Physically he was enormously attractive to women," says Jesse, an attribute he coupled with "a slick surface cleverness that enabled him to pass as rather a rough diamond of a gentleman in not too critical society." His motto, she suggested, could have been: "A single woman and her money are soon parted."

Leaving the army in 1887, Dougal supplemented his military pension with odd jobs in England and Ireland, everything from cutlery salesman to tavern keeper. This latter role ended in 1889 with the first of what would become a string of scrapes with the law. The tavern was badly damaged in a late-night fire, and Dougal made a claim for the insurance money. He was charged with arson, but acquitted at trial.

Dougal next turns up in London in the company of a woman named Emily Booty. She had only ninety pounds to her name, but it was enough for Dougal, who moved in with her and took over the finances. But he neglected to tell Booty that he already had a wife—his third—in Ireland. She found out soon enough, though, because Dougal invited his wife and children to move in. Incredibly, Booty endured these bizarre housekeeping arrangements for months before packing her bags. When Dougal, uttering threats, drove her from the house, she had him arrested for stealing the belongings she had been forced to leave behind. Dougal stood trial for theft in 1895, defending himself with a plea to the jury that a conviction would wipe out his military pension—fifty pounds a year. The jury took pity, finding Dougal not guilty but censuring his conduct in the affair.

Dougal's luck with the courts, however, was about to run out. Back in Ireland with his wife and children, Dougal was hired as a messenger at the Royal Hospital in Dublin. When cheques forged with the names of the hospital's administrators began turning up, Scotland Yard was called in. A detective traced the cheques to Dougal, who was convicted in January 1896 of forgery and uttering forged documents. Sentenced to twelve months at hard labour, Dougal promptly tried to hang himself. It was a half-hearted attempt, but it meant he would serve his time in a lunatic asylum instead of breaking rocks.

Stripped of his military pension, Dougal was a desperate man when he was released. And in 1898 he met the woman who would be his biggest meal ticket yet. Camille Cecile Holland, a prim, young-looking spinster in her mid-fifties, was elegant, refined, religious, virtuous—everything that Dougal was not. But it was not looks or character that attracted Dougal. Holland, thanks to an inheritance, had some 7,000 pounds in the bank. For a man like Dougal, it was like knowing the winning lottery numbers the day before the draw.

How Holland met the likes of Dougal remains a mystery. One story has her answering a newspaper personal ad. While that seems out of character for a proper Victorian lady, so does her conduct with Dougal. There is even evidence, from the few people in whom Holland confided, that she suspected Dougal was only after her money. But, believing she had found the love that had eluded her all her life, it was as if she were powerless to resist.

Nothing deterred her. Only weeks after they met, Holland moved in with Dougal, knowing full well he had a wife and family in Ireland. At his bidding, she bought the Moat Farm, so called because the main house was surrounded by a water-filled ditch like the castles of old. The couple moved in at the end of April 1899. Three weeks later, Holland told a servant that Dougal was driving her into the nearby town of Newport to do some shopping. It was the last time she was seen alive.

Dougal's wife arrived from Ireland and moved in the next day, helping herself to Holland's clothes and belongings. For four years Dougal lived the good life at Moat Farm, telling people who asked that Holland was visiting relatives or vacationing on the Continent. All the while he was cleaning out her bank accounts by forging her name on letters and cheques.

By the spring of 1902 Dougal's wife, fed up with his cruelty and constant adultery, moved out. In her place a succession of female servants passed through the household, adding to Dougal's growing list of conquests and illegitimate children. It was also the beginning of Dougal's undoing. The local rumour mill began working overtime, rife with stories of strange goings on at Moat Farm. Dougal, it was said, conducted bicycle riding lessons in secluded fields, with naked women as his students. And some began asking questions about what had happened to Holland; as the years went by, the possibility that she was away on vacation seemed increasingly remote. The local constable began making inquiries, and in March 1903 Dougal was arrested for forgery.

Immediately workmen began scouring the grounds of the Moat Farm. After five weeks of digging—and four years to the day after Holland's arrival at the estate—the body of a woman was uncovered near the main house. She had been shot once through the head, and crudely buried in a drainage ditch. The body was badly decomposed, but the clothing was identified as belonging to Holland. Dougal was charged with murder.

Was it the first time Dougal had resorted to murder in his long history of using and abusing women? Scotland Yard detectives had their suspicions, and began delving into his past. The trail lead to Halifax, where Dougal had spent eight of his twenty-one years in the military.

English heiress Camille Holland was Dougal's wealthiest victim, and his last. (*Chronicle-Herald/Mail-Star* files)

The Halifax newspapers were quick to make the connection once Dougal's murder and forgery charges hit the headlines. The *Morning Chronicle* noted in May 1903 that Dougal was remembered as "one of the finest looking men in uniform ever seen in Halifax," and "a great favourite with females." Considered "an ideal soldier," he had worked as chief clerk for the commanding officer of the Royal Engineers during his posting to Halifax and had been an avid yachtsman.

More intriguing was Dougal's marital history. He married his first wife, Lovenia Martha Griffiths, in March 1869, three years after entering the military and while still in England. He was twenty-two, she twenty-one. Griffiths accompanied him to Halifax, and the couple had four children. Her death in June, 1885 was sudden—by one account she fell ill and died within a day. She was buried two days later in Fort Massey cemetery in the city's south end.

Given compassionate leave to return to England, Dougal was back in Halifax within a matter of weeks with a new woman in tow. At twenty-eight, Mary Herberta Boyd was ten years Dougal's junior. The bereaved Dougal moved fast. On August 14 the couple was married at the home of the curate of St. Paul's Anglican Church. But by October 6, wife Number Two was also dead, and apparently with the same speed that claimed her predecessor. Dougal again arranged burial in Fort Massey cemetery.

Then a Halifax woman enters the picture. She became involved with Dougal not long after his second wife's death and went with him when he was posted to England in 1886. The couple had a child, but never married. The woman eventually left him and returned to Halifax.

In the wake of Dougal's arrest for murder, she was tracked down by an enterprising reporter for the Halifax *Evening Mail*. The woman, now in her late thirties and identified only as the wife of a civic employee, at first denied any knowledge of Dougal. But she invited the reporter into her home and was curious about the latest developments in the case. When the reporter asked point blank if she was the woman who had accompanied Dougal to England seventeen years earlier, she relented. "He was a monster," she said after a long silence, "and I was one of his victims."

Enamoured with Dougal's "great personal magnetism" and "handsome face," she said, she eloped with him to England. But Dougal kept putting off the marriage, and she moved in with a relative living in England. To save face with her family back home, she passed herself off as Mrs. Dougal for a time, then as his widow. She eventually returned to Halifax and married; her husband, she said, was the only one who knew the truth about her involvement with Dougal.

She did not mince words about her former lover. "Hanging is the proper death for Dougal," she told the *Evening Mail* reporter. "He should have suffered such a death long ago ... Dougal made the same false representations to the woman he is charged with murdering as he did to me ... and he has come to his end at last. May the monster get his deserts. I have no pity for him."

But the question remains: Was Dougal a multiple murderer? A check of Halifax probate records shows neither Lovenia Griffiths nor Mary Boyd left a will. Few women prepared wills in those days, and considering their ages—thirty-seven and twenty-eight respectively—it's not surprising the women had not taken that precaution. Without a will, their possessions would have passed on to Dougal—a possible motive for murder.

There is no record of an inquest into the death of either wife in Nova Scotia. As Tennyson Jesse points out, in the 1880s "a death that occurred in military quarters did not need to be registered in the civil part of town." Even if it had been, procedures were lax. In 1884, only months before Dougal became a widower twice in three months, a high-ranking Nova Scotia official noted that the provincial government kept no death records, and doubted there was such a registry anywhere in the province.

Under Canadian law coroners were empowered to convene a jury and hold an autopsy in cases of suspicious death, but such procedures were usually taken at the request of relatives of the deceased. Since Dougal's wives had come over with him from the United Kingdom, their families overseas were hardly in a position to doubt his word about how they died. Distance shielded Dougal from the kind of gossip that ultimately brought him to justice for the killing of Camille Holland.

Perhaps official indifference can be excused at the time of the deaths, when there was nothing to distinguish Dougal from the thousands of soldiers and sailors who passed through Halifax. But the 1903 reinvestigation is another story. By then Dougal was known to have a history of victimizing women, and in that context the sudden deaths of two wives in succession strike a sinister note.

The few Halifax police and Nova Scotia Attorney General's Department records that have survived for the period shed no light on the reinvestigation. But newspaper accounts suggest little was learned beyond the bare outline provided by looking up marriage and death announcements. Both women had taken ill and died suddenly; if foul play was involved, poison would appear to be the likely culprit. Yet the bodies were not exhumed, even though traces of poison would have endured the passage of almost two decades. Today, almost a century later, the answers remain buried somewhere in Fort Massey cemetery.

Dougal stood trial for the murder of Camille Holland in June 1903. The evidence was circumstantial, but the Crown showed clearly that Dougal had motive and opportunity to commit murder, and knowledge she was dead—showing the latter by forging her name with impunity for four years. He was convicted and sentenced to death.

As the appointed hour drew near, Dougal issued a confession of sorts, maintaining that he had accidently shot Holland in the head with a revolver and concealed her body out of fear that no one would believe him. He had that much right—no one did. On the scaffold in Chelmsford prison, just before the lever was pulled, he was urged to admit his guilt. "Are you guilty or not guilty," the chaplain asked, then repeated the question. "Guilty," Dougal blurted out just as the hangman pulled the lever.

As for his role in the deaths of Lovenia Griffiths and Mary Boyd, that was a secret Dougal took to his grave.

Chapter 5

Assigning the blame

Benjamin Russell was only half dressed when the huge explosion shook the rooming house in south-end Halifax. The other residents of the house, convinced the blast had been caused by "a bomb from the sky," appealed to Russell to join them in the safety of the basement. But curiosity drove the sixty-eight-year-old Supreme Court judge to the front door.

From his vantage point near the corner of Barrington and Morris Streets, Russell stood transfixed by the spectacle to the north. "A gently curving column of fire, of all the colors that fire can assume, was ascending from the region of the [naval] Dockyard, spreading and becoming wider and wider as it rose in height."

It was shortly after nine on the morning of December 6, 1917, and Russell had a ringside seat to the biggest man-made blast before the atomic age. After colliding with the freighter *Imo* in The Narrows of Halifax Harbour, the French munitions ship *Mont Blanc* had caught fire and had exploded, killing and maiming thousands and laying waste to large sections of Halifax and Dartmouth.

Russell's room was littered with shattered glass when he returned to finish dressing. Rumours that fires threatened to ignite the magazines at the Dockyard and cause a second explosion drove many south to the safety of Point Pleasant Park. Russell, a scholarly looking man in his well-groomed white beard, collected his private secretary and joined the exodus. Removed from the carnage and destruction in the city's north

57

end, the gathering among Point Pleasant's stately pines took on a carnival atmosphere. "A congenial company collected in the Park, to whom the hours passed swiftly," Russell recalled.

But it was not long before the reality of what had happened was driven home. Russell spent the evening looking for his brother John, a waterfront official, finally finding him in Victoria General Hospital. Luckily, he had suffered only minor injuries. The following morning, Russell was back at the hospital, where he volunteered to look after the growing number of homeless children. The designated room was a mess; every window was smashed, and snow covered the floor. Rolling up his sleeves, Russell cut up a roll of rubberized material he had purchased and nailed it over the windows. When a steamer arrived from Boston a few days later with clothing and other relief supplies, he designated the hallways of the Spring Garden Road courthouse as a drop-off point for the goods. But in the months ahead, Russell would play a pivotal role in the aftermath of the explosion as a judge, not as a relief worker.

"There was no upheaval of nature on that awful day," the *Halifax Herald* noted. "No enemy sent a shell hurtling into the city." But who was to blame? Who was responsible for the destruction rained on a city that, although no stranger to war, was far removed from the horrors of the trenches?

Rumours were rampant that the explosion was the work of German saboteurs. On December 10, Halifax police rounded up and jailed local citizens of German descent. The anti-German hysteria that gripped the crippled city was reflected in the newspapers. "So long as there are people in Halifax who remember this past week, or whose children remember it," the *Herald* predicted six days after the explosion, "so long will the name of Germany be a name for loathing and disgust." At one point the search for a scapegoat centred on the helmsman of *Imo*, a Norwegian named Johan Johansen, who suffered leg injuries in the explosion. Police, believing a letter found in his possession was written in German, promptly placed him under arrest. But hopes the perpetrator had been found were dashed within days—

Johansen was freed after it was determined that the writing was Norwegian, not German.

Finally, a commission of inquiry was set up by the federal minister of marine to get to the bottom of the disaster. It was the first step in a long effort to assign the blame and bring those responsible to justice. The explosion had done its deadly work in an instant; the legal fallout would take months to settle.

German saboteurs, real or imaginary, were not the only possible culprits. Suspicion fell on the men who brought *Mont Blanc*'s lethal cargo into Halifax. The munition ship's thirty-eight-year-old French skipper, Capt. Aime Le Medec, and local pilot Frank Mackey, forty-five, knew an explosion was inevitable and fled their burning ship after the collision. For many, their survival in the face of such widespread destruction confirmed their guilt. Fingers were also pointed at the official who had permitted *Mont Blanc* to enter the harbour, Commander Frederick Evans Wyatt. As chief examining officer for the Port of Halifax, Wyatt was responsible for monitoring the movements of all vessels entering and leaving Halifax.

The commission began its work a week after the explosion in the Halifax courthouse. The chairman was Mr. Justice Arthur Drysdale, who was assisted by two nautical assessors. A former attorney general in the Liberal government, Drysdale held the dual posts of judge of the Supreme and Admiralty courts. At sixty, he was in his tenth year on the bench. From the start, writer Michael J. Bird pointed out in his account of the explosion, *The Town That Died*, the judge "showed a bias in favour of *Imo*."

Questioning witnesses called before the commission were two of the ablest lawyers in the city. Humphrey Mellish, who appeared for the owners of *Mont Blanc*, was the "acknowledged leader" of the Nova Scotia bar, according to one observer. "His knowledge of the law is almost an institution." On the opposing side was C.J. Burchell, acting for *Imo*'s owners. "He was to prove, throughout the inquiry, capable of the most ruthless courtroom tactics and was constantly to attack and browbeat witnesses," noted Bird.

The first witnesses were Capt. Le Medec and pilot Mackey. The two men agreed on the events leading up to the collision, testifying that *Mont Blanc* proceeded up the Dartmouth side of the harbour, in accordance with the rules of navigation, until its course was intercepted by *Imo*. Despite a series of whistle signals and manoeuvres designed to ward off a collision, the larger freighter sliced into the hold of *Mont Blanc*, setting its volatile cargo ablaze.

On cross-examination, Burchell established that the ship was not flying a red warning flag, a precaution Le Medec insisted was required only during the loading or unloading of explosives. *Imo*'s lawyer also asked about the language barrier between the pilot and captain. "We spoke mostly in signs," Le Medec admitted, testifying through an interpreter, but "everything was clear between us." Burchell took a more aggressive stance in questioning Mackey, accusing the pilot of lying to the court and

The Belgian relief ship *Imo* ran aground on the Dartmouth side of Halifax harbour after the Mont Blanc exploded. (*Chronicle-Herald/Mail-Star* files)

of being a heavy drinker. But Mackey, a pilot with twenty-four years experience and an accident-free record prior to the collision, denied the accusations.

Survivors from *Imo*, including helmsman Johansen, gave a conflicting version of events leading up to the collision. *Imo* altered its course down the Halifax side of the harbour to avoid an incoming American steamer, then was forced to steer even closer to the Dartmouth shore by a tugboat towing barges. *Mont Blanc* was sighted and appeared to be passing to starboard when it veered across *Imo*'s path.

But *Imo* should not have been in The Narrows in the first place. Wyatt took the witnesses stand and said he had not authorized the ship to leave its anchorage in Bedford Basin. Although pilots were supposed to keep him informed of vessel clearances, Wyatt admitted this was not always done. Experienced pilots were in short supply to cope with the port's wartime vessel traffic, and no one could afford to crack down on those who broke the rules.

The commission closed its hearings on January 28, 1918. A week later Drysdale delivered his findings. Despite the conflicting evidence, the judge laid the blame for the collision squarely on *Mont Blanc*. That ship alone, he concluded, had caused the collision by violating the rules of the road. Mackey was accused of "gross negligence," and the judge recommended he be dismissed as a pilot and prosecuted under the criminal law. Le Medec likewise should have his master's licence cancelled and be "dealt with according to the law of his country." Both men were also rapped for "neglect of the public safety" by not warning the city's inhabitants of the impending explosion. Wyatt, Drysdale concluded, had neglected his duty to monitor vessel movements in the harbour.

Attorney General Orlando T. Daniels needed little prodding to lower the boom on *Mont Blanc*'s officers. He had already issued a warrant for the arrest of the captain and pilot on charge of manslaughter, naming *Imo*'s pilot, William Hayes, as the specific victim. Mackey, who sat in court as Drysdale read his decision, was arrested as he left the courthouse. Le Medec was

61

picked up a short time later as he walked through downtown Halifax. The pair were arraigned and ordered detained unless they could raised substantial bail— $10,000 for the captain, $6,000 for the pilot.

The *Herald* whole-heartedly endorsed the commission's ruling. "There are no ambiguities, there is no pussyfooting ... the conclusions are concisely stated in clear cut concrete language with a decisiveness and fearlessness that everyone expected from Mr. Justice Drysdale." But the arrests only whetted the paper's appetite for more. "The Halifax Herald also demands the immediate arrest of Commander Wyatt so that he can be placed on trial for his responsibility in the frightful catastrophe."

The call was heeded on February 5, the day the editorial appeared. Under instructions from the attorney general, police arrested Wyatt at his Edward Street home and brought him to court just in time for the preliminary hearing for Le Medec and Mackey. After Wyatt's bail was set at $6,000, a magistrate began hearing evidence against the trio in the grand jury room of the courthouse. The setting was appropriate—the room still showed signs of damage from the explosion two months earlier. Cracked plaster and a boarded-up window "combined to make up a dismal setting for one of the most important chapters in a great tragedy," wrote a *Herald* reporter with a flair for melodrama.

Prosecuting the case was Andrew Cluney. Walter J. O'-Hearn, a thirty-eight-year-old Halifax lawyer, appeared for Mackey while Wyatt chose to watch the proceedings without counsel. Mellish acted for *Mont Blanc*'s captain on the opening day of the preliminary hearing, a Tuesday, but was appointed to the Supreme Court over the weekend. Hector McInnis, Mellish's former law partner, picked up Le Medec's case.

The preliminary hearing was brief. Most testimony came from *Imo*'s crew, but one witness, not heard by the commission of inquiry, shed new light on the collision. The captain of a tug berthed at the naval dockyard testified that *Imo* caused the collision by changing course at the last minute. Despite the new evidence, all three accused were ordered to stand trial before the Supreme Court.

Benjamin Russell, a judge of the Nova Scotia Supreme Court, resisted public pressure to find scapegoats for the Halifax explosion. (Public Archives of Nova Scotia/Photograph collection)

O'Hearn wasted no time taking the case before a Supreme Court judge. Mr. Justice Benjamin Russell was asked to release Mackey, who was unable to raise bail and remained in custody, on a writ of *habeas corpus*. Russell was deeply troubled by the case. "It seemed to me that, so far from being negligent or careless ... the defendant had taken every possible care to prevent the collision which was about to be caused by the conduct of *Imo*," Russell recalled in his memoirs, displaying the same compassion he showed in the days following the explosion. "It surely cannot have been manslaughter for a defendant to have done what was best in his judgment to prevent an impending accident even if, in spite of his best efforts, the struggle was unsuccessful." Taking exception to the findings of Drysdale, a judge three years his junior on the bench, he ruled there was no evidence to support a criminal charge. Russell quashed the order to stand trial and directed that Mackey be released. The ruling also applied to Le Medec.

Meanwhile, on March 19 Wyatt's case went to a grand jury empanelled to decide if there was sufficient evidence to warrant a trial. Russell was again on the bench, and he reiterated his view that the evidence against Wyatt "fell short of the requirements for an indictment for manslaughter." With the grand jury as his audience, the judge then explained his rationale for discharging and *Mont Blanc*'s captain and pilot. Mackey could not be held criminally negligent for an error in judgment made "under circumstances in which the most careful and painstaking navigator could easily have been misled." As for Le Medec, it would have been "absurd" to hold him criminally responsible because the ship, once in the harbour, was in the hands of the pilot.

Russell had good reason to feel he was on the defensive. The clamour for revenge coming from outside the walls of his courtroom had already hit home. In the wake of the decision freeing *Mont Blanc*'s captain and pilot, someone speaking to one of Russell's sons on the street, but unaware of the relationship, ventured the opinion that the judge should be castrated for his ruling.

"When a great calamity such as that which has visited this city occurs," Russell told the jury, "there is a very natural and pardonable disposition ... to demand vengeance and seek to hold somebody criminally responsible.... It is quite possible that the injured feelings of the community should now be concentrated upon the naval official," Wyatt.

He was right. Ignoring the judge's instructions to throw out the case, the twenty-four-member grand jury returned a true bill sending Wyatt to trial. "To suppose that he had anything in the world to do with the disaster was an utterly lunatic notion," Russell later complained. "It was simply nonsensical, and the fact that a grand jury could find [a true bill] was symptomatic of the condition of the common feeling."

Prosecutor Cluney, perhaps buoyed by the outcome, announced that the Crown would appeal to the full bench of the Supreme Court to overturn the *habeas corpus* order granted Mackey and Le Medec. At the appeal heard April 2, the pilot's lawyer, O'Hearn, argued the court had no jurisdiction to disturb Russell's decision. A majority of the four-member court agreed and threw out the appeal. Not surprisingly, Drysdale was the lone voice in dissent.

The Crown refused to give up. Cluney was back in court April 9, this time seeking permission to prefer an indictment to bring Mackey before a grand jury. But the prosecutor was up against a brick wall in the form of Russell, who was still the judge presiding over the sitting of the grand jury. O'Hearn was first on his feet, objecting to the Crown's procedure and charging there was "an element of persecution" in the pursuit of his client. But Cluney contended he had fresh evidence bearing on the way *Mont Blanc* was navigated.

"Showing the pilot made a mistake?" Russell snapped. "Do we not all make mistakes? Is a man to be sent to the penitentiary for making a mistake?"

The judge handed down his decision the following day, refusing to put the case before the grand jury and calling the Crown's motion "an absolute absurdity." He likened Mackey's position to that of a surgeon losing a patient on the operating table, then having other doctors rule his actions "ill-advised" after an autopsy and leisurely study. Then he drove his point home by asking the jurors to trade places with the pilot. "Would they not think that they had already suffered sufficiently without being indicted as criminals for what at the very worst was an error in judgment?"

All that remained was Wyatt's trial on April 17. It lasted less than a day and the evidence, despite Cluney's promise, shed no new light on the collision. Russell, again on the bench, told the twelve-man trial jury there was "nothing in the eyes of the law" to justify the manslaughter charge. This time the judge had a jury willing to listen to him; the jurors acquitted Wyatt after only a few minutes of deliberation. The Crown did not appeal.

The civil courts also failed to find a legal scapegoat for the disaster. In Admiralty Court, Drysdale supported his earlier ruling at the commission stage, of course, finding that *Mont Blanc* had been at fault and awarding two million dollars in damages to *Imo*'s owners. But that decision was overturned on appeal all the way to the Supreme Court of Canada, which ruled that the ships were equally liable for the collision.

"WHO IS GUILTY?" asked a *Herald* editorial the day after Wyatt's acquittal. "It now seems as if the whole matter is to be forgotten; that all the investigation has been in vain and that the responsibility for what was undoubtedly one of the most ghastly blunders the world has ever known, is never going to be fixed."

Mackey, suspended in the wake of the commission's findings, was eventually reinstated as a pilot. Le Medec continued to command vessels for *Mont Blanc*'s owners until 1922; he retired in 1931. Wyatt, although cleared of criminal charges, was transferred from Halifax to a less sensitive post. And Russell, who had worked overtime to prevent the three men from taking the fall for the explosion, retired from the bench in 1924, at age seventy-five. He made one last defence of his rulings on the explosion cases in his autobiography published in 1932, three years before his death.

Chapter 6

Holocaust at the Queen Hotel

Ted Mitchell never figured out what woke him the winter morning Halifax's Queen Hotel burned to the ground. "The smoke was coming through the transom," he recalled. "There was a roar, I didn't know what it was, in the hallway. I had sense enough to keep the door closed and go to the window."

He was trapped, three stories up. Fire was rapidly engulfing the hotel, fire trucks were pulling up, and people were screaming for help as firefighters and passersby frantically tried to reach them with ladders. Mitchell, a forty-nine-year-old salesman, either jumped or fell. "I was on the window sill, that's the last thing I remember till I came to on the ground." He was lying on the pavement on the waterfront side of the hotel, unable to move.

"You're all right now, you're out of the fire," said one of the men who came to his aid. Mitchell was carried to a store on Lower Water Street, where the proprietor, an elderly woman, looked after him. "I wanted a drink of water and the old lady was very kind and very much concerned about the situation, so she gave me a drink of milk. The next thing was, police cars came along, and I remember someone saying: 'You better take this fellow, he's hurt pretty bad'." Mitchell, both legs and an arm broken in the fall, was put in the back seat of a cruiser and rushed to Victoria General Hospital. It would be fourteen months before he was well enough to walk out the hospital door.

Mitchell was lucky to escape with his life. Twenty-eight people died in the blaze on the early morning of March 2, 1939. Out of almost ninety guests and employees in the hotel at the

67

time of the fire, another nineteen people were injured, suffering burns, cuts, broken bones and shock. The hotel and two adjoining buildings were razed, causing an estimated $800,000 damage. The Queen Hotel fire was Halifax's worst in half a century, and was described in the press of the day as the worst disaster to befall the city since the explosion of 1917.

"Hollis Street looked as if it had been ripped by a tornado," the *Halifax Herald* reported the morning after the tragedy. "Debris littered the street, and all lanes of traffic were blocked by fire apparatus ... The skeleton walls of the once-famous hotel were reminiscent of scenes in battle-scarred France."

Controversy fanned by the fire burned long after the last ember had been extinguished. The inferno raised questions about fire safety in hotels, schools, theatres and public buildings across Nova Scotia, and revealed shocking lapses in the enforcement of fire regulations. A public inquiry and a royal commission were set up to probe the disaster, culminating in the prosecution of the hotel's owner in the criminal courts on a charge of wilfully causing the fatal fire.

In its heyday, the Queen was one of Halifax's top hotels. The site on the east side of Hollis Street, between Sackville and Salter streets, was first occupied by the International Hotel, which burned down in the 1870s without loss of life. The hotel was rebuilt, and purchased in 1886 by A.B. Sheraton, a New Brunswick businessman who, despite his surname, had no experience in the hotel trade. Sheraton, described as "enterprising and impulsive," resolved to turn the rather dilapidated premises into a first-rate hotel. By 1890 he had spent more than $70,000 to renovate and buy new furniture, renaming it the Queen Hotel. The result was a posh hotel—and a massive debt. Sheraton's backers foreclosed, and after a messy court battle had him ejected from the premises. The shareholders leased the hotel to J.P. Fairbanks, who bought the property in 1901.

The Queen and its Hollis Street neighbour, the Halifax Hotel, were the luxury hotels of their time. Hollis Street was the heart of Halifax's business district, only a short walk from the waterfront that was the lifeblood of a city built on trade. The Queen boasted

At the turn of the century, the posh Queen was one of Halifax's finest hotels. (*Chronicle-Herald/Mail-Star* files)

two large, mirror-lined dining rooms for meetings and luncheons. A roof garden, shaded by awnings, offered a commanding view of the harbour and a cool oasis in the summer. Located only two blocks south of Province House, it was popular haunt for politicians in town for the sitting of the legislature. Thomas Raddall, in his chronicle of Halifax's history, *Warden of the North*, says it was widely believed that more government business was transacted at the Queen than in Province House itself.

Renovation and expansion turned the Queen into a rambling, ninety-three-room hotel with three distinct sections. The lobby, elevators, newsstand and hotel offices were in the original, five-storey wooden structure. On the south side was a five-storey addition built in 1908 of concrete, with offices at street level, bedrooms and baths on the upper floors. At the rear, stretching towards the harbour as far as Upper Water Street, was a section containing the kitchen, dining rooms, furnace room and three floors of bedrooms.

By 1930, the Queen was past its prime. A building permit was obtained that year to carry out renovations, but the work was never done. The Depression was no time to pump scarce money into the upkeep of a hotel. Even though the Queen was beginning to show its age, it still attracted some of the better guests. R.T. Caldwell, the former Tory MLA for Kings County and a member of the province's board of censors, was a permanent resident. So was Arthur DeWitt Foster, another Kings County Tory who had caused a minor scandal during the First World War by acting as the Militia Department's purchasing agent for horses while sitting as a government MP. In all, about forty-five people called the Queen home.

Ted Mitchell of Bridgewater, who travelled around the province selling tinned milk for the Nestle company, used to work Halifax in two- to three-week stints. "I always stayed at the Queen Hotel when I was working in the city," he recalled. The hotel seemed as safe as any. "I had no troubles with the Queen Hotel, [it was] a good old hotel under the conditions."

In June 1936, at the height of the Depression, Halifax businessman John Simon paid a paltry $17,500 for the Queen. The price was so good, he bought the property without bothering to inspect its condition. "I was satisfied, knowing the property," he explained. Simon knew a good buy when he saw one. After arriving in the city in 1896 at age twenty, he had built a successful firm dealing in scrap metal, then diversified into shipping on a modest scale. Under the imposing name Hochelaga Shipping and Towing Company, he operated several small vessels; the flagship of the fleet was the *Hochelaga*, a combination cargo-passenger boat with a regular run between Pictou and Prince Edward Island. He also dabbled in real estate, and that brought him to the Queen.

Like Sheraton before him, Simon had no experience running a hotel. And he had trouble finding someone who did, going through four managers in less than three years. His son, Sydney, and a daughter, Ida, helped out, but day-to-day decisions like staffing and minor purchases were left up to the manager.

Simon would contend he had pumped $30,000 into repairing the hotel by 1939, but that claim seems unlikely; the building and furniture combined were insured for only $33,000. With business slow everywhere, it was a time for cost-cutting, not capital outlays. One of Simon's first acts as president of the Queen Hotel Company Limited was to trim the staff from about forty to twenty-nine, including cutting the night shift from four employees to two. He also trimmed salaries. But a smaller payroll did little to improve the bottom line; the hotel consistently operated in the red.

Wednesday, March 1, 1939. This was the day John Desmond would rid himself of Victor Bouffard. Desmond, an officious, experienced manager who had been in charge at the Queen Hotel for a number of months, was fed up with Bouffard's drinking on duty. As one of the hotel's firemen, Bouffard was responsible for stoking the furnace with coal and patrolling the building on the night shift, but most of the time he was drunk. "Dirty drunk," Desmond called it.

The dismissal had been cleared with the owner. After all, Bouffard had come to the Queen after working as a deckhand on one of Simon's boats, and knew the boss. When Bouffard picked up his pay envelope that afternoon, inside was a note giving him two-weeks notice.

"I started to celebrate," recalled Bouffard, a heavy-set man with a hook nose and a full head of black hair. He bought two bottles of scotch, downed one, went to a restaurant for a meal and drank the other. About nine in the evening, he rolled into lobby of the Queen and gave Desmond a piece of his mind. "If I'm out of a job, then there's going to be a lot more looking for a job tomorrow," he threatened, then babbled something about seeing Desmond in Dorchester penitentiary "and I'll laugh at you." Desmond fired Bouffard on the spot and told him to clear out of the hotel.

Bouffard staggered off, polished off a third bottle of liquor, and returned to the hotel after Desmond went to bed. The night desk clerk, Eddie Weaver, let him stay, fearing Bouffard "might start a row." Besides, Weaver could use the help. The night clerk was severely overworked: he was supposed to man the desk and switchboard, operate the elevator, clean the lobby, patrol the building and duck out for food for the guests. Despite Bouffard's condition, when he offered to run the elevator, Weaver agreed.

About two in the morning, a guest who had lived at the hotel for twenty years, Harvey Putman, called the switchboard. He thought he smelled smoke. Weaver roused Desmond and they traced the smoke to a janitor's closet on the second floor of the hotel's rear section, four floors above the furnace room. Inside, they found a newspaper burning in a garbage can. Weaver pulled the can into the hall and used an extinguisher to douse the flames. The closet wall had been scorched, but there was no other damage. The fire had obviously been set—burnt paper matches were lying on the floor.

Desmond had a good idea who the culprit was. Bouffard had been on the elevator a half hour earlier; they found him passed out in a chair in the lobby. Despite his suspicions, Desmond left Bouffard there and did not report the incident to the fire department. Desmond went back to his room in the hotel to sleep. But the fire had rattled Weaver, who stepped up his patrols of the building to every half hour. "I was just uneasy," he explained. So was the guest who had smelled smoke. Putman got dressed and hung around the lobby for almost an hour before returning to his room.

A poker game in Room 166 broke up about three-thirty in the morning and the four players headed for bed. Weaver, the only one left awake in the building, went into the hotel office about five-thirty to write a letter. A few minutes later, Bouffard woke up in the lobby, "feeling kind of seedy," as he put it. He had no recollection of his run-in with Desmond, or how he had ended up sleeping in the lobby. Thirsty and hung over, he bought a bottle of ginger ale from Weaver and headed downstairs to the furnace room to pick up his belongings.

He smelled smoke in the stairwell. Just the furnace, he thought. But when he passed the furnace room, he saw no smoke. "That struck me as funny," Bouffard recalled. He went into the next room and woke up the day fireman, Arthur Caldwell, then headed upstairs to see where the smoke was coming from. He got as far as the landing. The floor between the furnace room and the lobby was filled with smoke and Bouffard could see flames licking at the walls. Caldwell was getting dressed as Bouffard burst into his room.

"Great God!" he shouted. "Get up. There's a fire!" By now the furnace room was thick with smoke. Caldwell went inside, turned off the boilers to prevent an explosion, and woke up other staff members who lived at the rear of the hotel. He and Bouffard escaped by breaking a window overlooking an alley.

Upstairs, headwaitress Sophie Martell had gone to the lobby to check the guest list to find out how many people to expect for breakfast. It was about twenty minutes past six. As she turned to go back to the dining room, smoke began to billow into the lobby. "It was so thick I couldn't get through," she said. Weaver stuck his head out of the hotel office. "Oh God, Sophie!" he yelled. "A fire!" He ran to the switchboard, called the fire department, then tried to awaken guests by calling their rooms. He got through to one man before the heavy smoke drove him out of the building.

Charles Lynch, a twenty-year-old cub reporter for the *Herald* and *Mail*, was walking past the hotel after working the night shift. The air was cold but there was no snow—a typical late winter day in Halifax. Suddenly a curtain of fire swept out of the front of the hotel, shattering the lobby's large windows.

The first fire trucks were on the scene within minutes, but the fire spread with deadly speed. The hotel's elevator shaft was not fireproof, giving the flames a path to the upper floors. Flames and smoke quickly turned the upstairs hallways into a deathtrap. People unable to flee their rooms on the upper floors stood at their windows screaming for help. Some tried to climb down knotted bedsheets. Below, firefighters dropped their hoses and concentrated on putting up ladders to rescue them. But their efforts were hampered by a tangle of overhead power lines and trolley cables. Even worse, not even the fire department's single aerial ladder could reach the top floor.

Heroes were made that morning. One was Clyde MacIntosh, the Queen's daytime desk clerk. He awoke in his fourth-floor room about six-thirty, choking on smoke. Jumping onto the fire escape outside his window, he began pounding on windows to

A Halifax firefighter perched on a ladder helps a guest from an upper floor of the burning Queen Hotel. (*Chroncicle-Herald/Mail-Star* files)

wake guests. He helped nine people down the fire escape, the last an unconscious man he carried over his shoulders to safety. The iron rungs on the fire escape were so hot they were burning his feet, but MacIntosh scurried back up. He reached the third floor but was overcome by smoke and toppled onto the pavement below. Incredibly, he was not seriously injured.

Other scenes were etched forever on the memories of sur-vivors and rescuers alike. Robert Murray, the former sheriff of Cumberland County, made it to the street, but ran back into the burning building to save his wife. Both perished. One woman grabbed at a nearby ladder, missed, and was left suspended from a window ledge as firefighters used their hoses to beat back the flames. Two firefighters climbed the ladder and managed to put a rope under her arms just as she lost consciousness.

About a dozen people jumped to the roof of the hotel's rear section, but fell to their deaths when it collapsed into the inferno below. A man named Elliff dropped his two young children into a life net thirty feet below. "It was a terrible feeling," he confessed later. "but it was the only thing to do." The children were unharmed. One firefighter clambered through a window and, silhouetted against the flames, saw the figure of a woman kneel-ing in prayer. A rush of searing heat drove him back to the window before he could reach her.

By mid-morning it was all over. Lynch, who had stood transfixed as the drama unfolded in front of him, rushed back to his office to help get out an extra of the afternoon paper. It was a scoop. The fire cut power to the offices of the *Chronicle*, and the rival paper was unable to run its presses.

Initial reports put the death toll as high as fifty, but that number was reduced to twenty-eight after the hotel register was recovered from a safe in the ruins. The dead included former politicians Caldwell and Foster, retired provincial engineer Rod McColl, and the Cuban consul. Many of the bodies were so badly burned they could only be identified through dental records. Ten were never identified.

The legislature adjourned for the day out of respect for the dead, after Premier Angus L. Macdonald moved a resolution of sympathy for the victims and their families. Telegrams of con-dolence poured in as news of the holocaust flashed around the globe. Within hours of the fire, a telegram arrived at city hall from King George VI, who assured the people of Halifax that his government joined "in the general expression of sympathy which this catastrophe will evoke throughout the entire country."

There were immediate calls for a full investigation of the tragedy. "Let it be probed to the bottom," proclaimed a front-page editorial in the *Halifax Mail*. "There must be a full and far-reaching investigation," demanded the New Glasgow *Evening News*, "it will likely be found that many other buildings used for the same purpose throughout the province are equally dangerous." Opposition Leader P.C. Black called on the provincial government to launch an inquiry. "I have been informed ... that there may not have been adequate fire escape protection in the burned hotel," he charged.

The outcry sparked two public inquiries. The fire marshal opened an investigation on March 6; within days the government appointed a royal commission, headed by Mr. Justice M.B. Archibald of the Supreme Court, with a mandate to probe not only the Queen Hotel fire, but also the state of fire prevention in the province.

Testimony of survivors and hotel staff at the inquiries revealed that the Queen broke virtually every fire regulation on the books. There were no ropes in the rooms; there was no fire alarm to awaken guests; the iron fire escapes had wooden landings that quickly burned away in the fire; there were no signs in the rooms to show the direction to the fire escapes, and, besides, access was through private rooms that were likely locked; and none of the staff members had been told what to do in case of a fire. The only redeeming feature was the presence of fire extinguishers, two to a floor, all apparently in working order.

It became increasingly obvious that responsibility for the almost total lack of safety measures lay with one man—John Simon. "From the day I stepped into the hotel, I did everything possible [to prevent a fire]," the owner testified at one of the inquiries. "I always employed first-class mechanics on that kind of work." But, when pressed, Simon admitted his only action in that line had been to hire a man to chip rust from the fire escapes and paint them.

Simon had found it easy to ignore safety laws because they were not enforced. The inquiries exposed a legacy of neglect and inaction by the officials responsible for inspecting buildings and ensuring fire regulations were followed. Nova Scotia hotels, it turned out, were the responsibility of the factories inspector, Phillip Ring, whose policy was to check a hotel only when he received a complaint. Ring had inspected all Halifax hotels in 1937 at the request of the provincial minister of labour. Violations of fire safety laws were noted in writing, but there was no follow-up to see if hotelkeepers corrected the problems.

Ring's dealings with the Queen illustrated the danger of that policy. He inspected the hotel in March 1937, and ordered four steps be taken immediately to conform with the hotel fire safety act: install ropes in each room; repair handrails on the fire escapes; post signs in the hallways to show the location of fire escapes; and post similar notices in each room. Ring sent a letter to the hotel management containing those instructions, but never returned to ensure they were carried out. Asked why he did not prosecute, Ring offered a weak explanation: the hotel's manager at the time, E.E. Amirault, had been a friend from childhood and he trusted him to comply with the letter.

Amirault testified he had personally read the letter to Simon, who had directed the manager to fix the handrails and to ignore the other instructions. Amirault's version of events was corroborated by the handyman who repaired the fire escapes. Simon, for his part, denied ever seeing the letter.

Hearings continued into the late spring of 1939, but reports of the testimony were often swept off the front pages by the bleak news of a world on the brink of war. Archibald delivered the royal commission's report in November, coming down hard on fire safety officials. The legislation was there, he ruled; what was needed was a vigorous, co-ordinated effort to enforce those laws. He called for a revamped fire marshal's office, directly responsible to the government and armed with more power to enforce fire regulations. As for the Halifax Fire Department, the judge reported that it was undermanned and its equipment was outdated and inadequate. The aerial ladder, dating from 1919, was so rickety the fire chief had warned his men that they used it at their own risk.

The judge could not determine from the evidence the exact cause of the fire. It had apparently started just above the furnace room, possibly where unprotected pipes from the furnace came too close to the wooden ceiling. Another suggestion was that an ember from the early-morning fire in the janitor's closet had dropped down the wall, and smouldered for several hours before starting a new fire. The judge's report made no mention of Bouffard's threat or the suspicion that he had set that earlier fire. "There is nothing in the evidence to justify the conclusion that the fire was deliberately set," he wrote.

But Archibald left no doubt where responsibilty for the fire lay. Simon called the shots at the hotel, and the judge was satisfied he had seen the 1937 letter outlining safety measures to be taken. "The person responsible for this non-compliance with the inspector's requirements was John Simon."

Halifax police had begun questioning members of the Queen Hotel staff, including Vic Bouffard, while firefighters were still pouring water over the building's smouldering ruins. Little more than two weeks after Archibald tendered his report, and in accordance with his findings, a charge of wilfully causing a fire through negligence was laid against the sixty-three-year-old scrap dealer-turned-hotelkeeper.

It was believed to be the first prosecution in Canada under a section of the Criminal Code, introduced in 1919, that made owners of burned buildings criminally responsible for causing fires if they had not taken proper safety measures. An owner was "deemed to have caused the fire through negligence," the section held, if he had "failed to obey the requirements of any law intended to prevent fires" and if loss of life or property "would not have occurred if such law had been complied with." A conviction could bring up to five years in prison.

Simon's health was not good—he was ill at home at the time of the hotel fire—and the preliminary hearing was adjourned several times because he was too sick to come to court. Finally, in October 1940, with all the evidence in, he was ordered to stand

Queen Hotel owner John Simon wound up in the criminal courts, charged with failing to take measures to prevent the fire that claimed twenty-eight lives. (*Chronicle-Herald/Mail-Star* files)

trial on the charge. The case went to county court in January 1941. The judge was Robert H. Murray, an outspoken, progressive-minded former Crown prosecutor. "A kindly soul—a friend of humanity who was known for his keen sense of humour and conversant with the problems that beset mankind," recalled one Halifax lawyer who knew him well.

79

The events leading up to the fire had been well-sifted by previous inquiries, so the Crown concentrated on the deaths of three guests in making its case against Simon. They included John Johnson, who was passing through Halifax after refereeing a hockey game in the Annapolis Valley and checked into the Queen just hours before the fire broke out. The three victims had been in the part of the building farthest from the area where the fire started, making them the most likely to have escaped if proper fire safety equipment had been installed.

Murray mulled over the evidence for two weeks before handing down his ruling. He took a dim view of how Simon had run his business. "It is safe to say that, like many other hotels in the province, the company had not conformed to the laws made for the safeguarding of guests from the hazards of fire," he said when court reconvened on January 30, 1941. "No doubt the protection of dollars rather than that of human life received the greatest consideration .... The hotel was run at a comparatively heavy loss which was not an inspiration to the company to do anything further for the protection of the guests." With those thoughts out of his system, Murray turned to the law. The Crown had established that Simon had been negligent in not complying with fire safety laws, but the section required proof that the fire and the deaths it caused "would not have occurred" if he had done so. Would ropes in the rooms, a central fire alarm, and signs in the rooms and hallways showing the location of fire escapes have saved Johnson and the others? Murray thought many of the twenty- eight victims would probably have been awakened by an alarm and escaped, "but in view of the criminal law a probability is not sufficient to convict. If the law read 'the loss of life *might* not have occurred' I may have been at liberty to draw a convincing inference ...." The case turned on a single word. The judge ruled he had to give the accused the benefit of the doubt and found Simon not guilty.

Simon's troubles were not over. He faced lawsuits from survivors and families of victims of the blaze; one action, seeking $5,600 in damages, was settled out of court for an undisclosed amount. He was also hauled back into court in April 1941, charged with breaching fire regulations by installing non-fire resistant shingles on a group of waterfront buildings. It reflected a new resolve on the part of officials, in the wake of the Queen Hotel disaster, to enforce fire safety laws. But Simon was acquitted because the Crown could not prove he owned the buildings—he was still negotiating to buy them when the charge was laid.

Simon died in a Halifax nursing home in April 1966. He was ninety. Charles Lynch earned a ten-dollar bonus for his fire scoop, and went on to become one of Canada's best-known political pundits. The Queen Hotel site lay vacant until the Bank of Canada erected a building in the late 1950s. And Ted Mitchell, who lived to be 101, recovered from his injuries and went back to selling milk. But his harrowing escape from the Queen Hotel was not soon forgotten.

"I used to check every hotel I'd go to. I'd see if there was a rope in the room," he recalled with a chuckle about a year before his death in 1990. "I went into one hotel, and I won't mention the name, and I said, 'Ropes in good order?' 'Oh, yes,' [the manager] said, 'there it is there.' So I picked it up and uncoiled it and dropped it out of the window. It went down about halfway to the pavement." Needless to say, Mitchell spent the night in another hotel.

Part Three

Cheating the hangman

John Ruff's body

At first, no one in the tiny community of Five Islands suspected that John Ruff, head of the only family on Moose Island, was the victim of foul play. The oldest of Ruff's six sons, Andrew, rowed to the mainland with the body on the last day of July 1842. The boys all told the same story. Ruff had been cutting a tree the day before and it fell on him, crushing his skull. Andrew attributed the delay in seeking help to the tide and his leaky rowboat.

The local magistrate, John Fulmore, saw no need to summon the coroner. He empanelled a jury and convened an inquiry that same afternoon. After examining the body and hearing unsworn testimony from Andrew Ruff, the jury returned a verdict of accidental death. John Ruff was buried on the mainland and his wife and sons gradually dispersed. Case closed.

It stayed closed for about two years, until eleven-year-old Ben Ruff began telling people a different story. He claimed that his brothers Arthur and Andrew had murdered their father in cold blood as he slept. As Andrew looked on, he said, Arthur had struck John Ruff on the head with the back of an axe. Was it murder or the product of a young boy's imagination? The authorities, armed with little more than Ben's word, decided to take no chances. Arthur could not be located, but Andrew was rounded up and charged with murder.

Only one hundred acres in size, Moose Island is the largest of five islands that jut into the Bay of Fundy at the foot of Economy Mountain. Micmac legend has it that the god Glooscap created the chain of islands by hurling great stones across the bay from the top of Cape Blomidon. The islands were named for their shape—Diamond, Long, Egg, Pinnacle and Moose, the last because it resembled the hump of a moose rising out of the water. Moose is the closest to the mainland, about a mile across the mud flats at low tide.

In the mid-1800s, it was also the only island with permanent residents. John Ruff, an Irishman, and his wife, Susannah, cleared and farmed about forty-five acres on Moose Island and raised six children. Isaiah and Noah had left home by 1842, but Andrew, Arthur, Benjamin, and Anthony still lived with their parents. Members of the family were frequent visitors to the mainland, no doubt to socialize and purchase supplies.

But the Ruffs were not a happy family. Susannah later claimed that her husband was "very harsh" and beat her often. He was also no stranger to drink. The day before his death, Ruff and his wife went to Five Islands; Susannah remained at the settlement and Ruff returned the following day, "not very sober" according to Ben. Only Andrew, Arthur, Ben and Anthony were on the island when their father died: just four people knew how Ruff came to his untimely death.

"If murder be a crime of great magnitude," James F. Gray told the jurors as he opened the Crown's case against Andrew Ruff, "how much more aggravated is its enormity when perpetrated against the parent who gave us existence. Yet, such is the nature of crime with which the prisoner is charged in this indictment." It was mid-October 1844, and Andrew was on trial before the Supreme Court in Truro for aiding and abetting the murder of his father.

Gray, in his twentieth year at the bar, had a reputation as "a very careful practitioner," said one colleague. During the tenure of his former law teacher, Samuel G. W. Archibald, as attorney-general, Gray was retained to handle at least two major prosecutions. In 1835, he and Archibald unsuccessfully prosecuted *Novascotian* editor Joseph Howe for libel. Three years later, Gray put together the circumstantial evidence needed to send Maurice

Doyle to the gallows for the brutal axe murder of Cumberland County farmer John Clem.

Given his extensive trial experience, Gray probably sensed that he could have a loser on his hands. His case rested squarely on the word of an eleven-year-old boy. The day before trial, Gray sent the coroner to Five Islands to exhume Ruff's body. But, after more than two years in the grave, the autopsy was inconclusive.

"The principal witness on the part of the Crown is but a lad, the brother of the prisoner," Gray told the jurors at the end of his opening address, laying his cards on the table. "And if you believe his testimony, you must find a verdict of guilty."

Ben Ruff was sworn to tell the truth and began his tale. Two years earlier, he said, his father returned from a trip to the mainland around hay mowing time. John Ruff had been drinking and "jawed a little" at the boys. After supper, Ruff went to a bed in the barn with Anthony to sleep.

"Arthur went and got the axe and struck father on the head," Ben told the court. "Andrew was standing by the mow but never struck him." But Andrew helped Arthur drag the body out of the barn and the pair cut down a tree to make the death look like an accident. Andrew also used an adze to chip bloodstained wood from the barn floor.

"They did not want to get Arthur hung," he explained matter-of-factly. "I cried all night and Arthur did not cry a bit." Ben also claimed his mother was aware of the murder. Soon after the slaying, he said, he took her to the barn and showed her where Ruff's blood had run between the floor boards.

For defence lawyer George R. Young, the task was clear. He must discredit the boy in the jury's eyes. Young began his cross-examination with questions about Ben's background. The boy could not read, had no formal schooling, and never attended church until he came to Truro after his father's death. His mother often accused him of telling lies, Ben acknowledged.

Then the lawyer turned to Andrew's role in the alleged killing. Ben admitted he did not hear his brother tell Arthur to get the axe, but added he must have or Arthur would not have done so. Ben also acknowledged that he did not hear Andrew tell Arthur to strike Ruff.

"Andrew was a very good boy," he continued. After the fatal blow was struck, "Andrew came out crying and was crying all night but Arthur did not cry." Ben again described Andrew's role in cleaning up after the murder, this time claiming it was Andrew's idea to make it look like an accident. "Andrew said they did not want to get Arthur hung and would cut a tree and let on it fell on him [Ruff]. Andrew was not afraid of getting hanged."

Young asked Ben to demonstrate how his father was lying when struck. Ben indicated the right side. During direct examination, in response to a question from a juror, Ben had said the left side. A minor discrepancy, something Young could build on in his closing arguments.

"We saw something very strange that night," Ben offered. For lawyers, asking a question without knowing the answer is a risky game, but Young decided to take a chance.

"What did you see?" the defence lawyer asked.

"I think it was the devil. It was black, it looked just like ..." Ben said, searching for words, "about as big as Mr. Craig's big dog."

Ben Ruff's bizarre statement came out of the blue. Everyone in the courtroom strained to hear the next words. Gray, watching his case slip away, probably buried his face in his hands.

"What did you do?" Young asked.

"We all got up on the mow. He came in and sat in one corner of the barn. He did not stop long."

"How did you know it was the devil?"

"We all thought it was the devil," Ben testified. "We saw the devil once before on the island."

"When was that?" asked Young, unable to believe his luck.

"My sister saw him behind the barrel when father was going to kill mother with a jackknife, but when he knew the devil was there he did not do it."

"Did you see the devil at other times?" Young asked, so eager to keep the witness talking he neglected to point out that Ben had no sisters.

"The devil was in the house another time," Ben complied. "We went to bed and did not leave any wood on the fire and when we got up in the morning we found a good fire on."

Satisfied that Ben's credibility was shattered, Young continued his line of questioning. Ben admitted that at other times he had told people his father's death was an accident. "I always told lies about it till I came to court. I know I will have to tell the truth here," he said.

"Did you ever tell anyone the death was not an accident?" asked Young.

Ben agreed he had, after hearing people say that the boys had killed their father. He admitted he told a Truro merchant that Arthur killed Ruff and Andrew had nothing to do with the crime. "I'm sure Andrew had nothing to do with killing him," Ben added, contradicting his earlier testimony.

The damage was done. Gray tried to patch a few of the holes on re-examination. "Were you frightened when you saw the devil?"

"We all were."

"Were you afraid when you saw your father lying dead?" the prosecutor asked, hoping the jurors would think the boy's strange vision had been brought on by a state of shock.

"Yes," Ben replied.

Finally, Ben said that Andrew was older than Arthur. Gray obviously wanted the jury to consider Andrew as a leader rather than a follower, and more likely to plan and cover up a murder.

Gray forged ahead. His next witness was magistrate Fulmore, who conducted the 1842 inquest into Ruff's death. "I had no suspicions he was murdered," he explained. Ruff's skull was indented and crushed above the ear. "The inference was that it was done by a knot on the tree." He attributed Andrew's one-day delay in bringing the body to the mainland to the tide and a leaky rowboat.

Mr. Justice William Blowers Bliss of the Nova Scotia Supreme Court lashed out at the authorities for failing to gather the evidence needed to determine how John Ruff died. (Painting hanging in the Halifax Law Courts/Author photo)

The presiding judge, Mr. Justice William Blowers Bliss, had heard enough. Interrupting the line of questioning, the judge sternly rebuked Fulmore for the "irregular" inquest. "An investigation of this nature did not come within the sphere of your duty," he said, reminding magistrates to call for a coroner in all cases of sudden death. "Had the proper officer been called at the time, his medical skill would have enabled him to elicit facts which would either have exculpated the parties charged or fastened the guilt upon them."

The judge hit the nail on the head. Rumours, unanswered questions, and the dubious testimony of an young boy could not overcome the lack of hard evidence. At best, the life of an innocent man had been put in jeopardy needlessly. At worst, shoddy investigation meant a murderer would go free.

The next Crown witnesses were two Five Islands men who examined the blown-down barn at the abandoned Ruff homestead. Both found what appeared to be blood on the floorboards and noted where a layer of wood had been chipped away. Pieces of bloodstained wood were shown to the jurors but, on cross-examination, Young established that it was common to slaughter cattle in barns.

The coroner, Dr. Waddell, was the prosecution's final witness. He exhumed Ruff's badly decomposed body at Five Islands the day before and confirmed a fracture to the left side of the skull. He concluded the injury could have been caused by a blow from a falling tree or the back of an axe.

With the Crown's star witness on the ropes, Young moved in for the kill. The defence called Susannah Ruff, who told the court her late husband often beat her. She described Andrew as "a good boy," but denounced Ben as "a bad boy" whose word was suspect. She denied that Ben ever told her John Ruff was murdered or showed her blood on the barn floor.

"Where is Arthur?" Gray asked on cross-examination, curious about the whereabouts of the missing co-accused. But Susannah Ruff was not about to let the Crown put another of her sons on trial. "Ben and Arthur left home together and Arthur has not returned. I heard he died in Halifax," she replied.

90

A Five Islands man, Charles McLellan, testified he went to Moose Island to help remove Ruff's body. It was lying near a fallen tree and there was blood on the bark. "Ruff was not a good chopper," he noted. Young closed the defence with a trio of witnesses who knew Ben Ruff and felt he could not be believed. "I do not think him of sound mind," said one. The jury agreed, finding Andrew not guilty after thirty minutes of deliberation. Based on the evidence, it was the only possible verdict.

It is said Ruff's ghost still haunts Moose Island, which has remained uninhabited in the century and a half since his death. But the legend is based on little more than a handful of reports of mysterious lights spotted from the mainland. The work of the devil, Ben Ruff might say.

Death at the Waterloo Tavern

The noisy taverns and brothels of Halifax's notorious Barrack Street area were closing down as city watchmen John Shehan and Maurice Power made their rounds. It was a few minutes past midnight on a damp, overcast September night in 1853. Suddenly, Thomas Murphy ran up to the officers. "Come quickly," he shouted. "A man has jumped out of a window of my house."

With the watchmen at his heels, Murphy ran back to the Waterloo Tavern, the establishment he operated just south of the Town Clock. A sailor, a crewman from a British man-of-war anchored in the harbour, was sprawled at the foot of the staircase leading into the tavern; his head, bloody from cuts above each eye, rested on the bottom step. Broken glass and a hat, handkerchief and a pair of shoes littered the sidewalk. There were no signs of life.

Shehan was told the man had fallen from one of the tavern's second-storey windows—a distance of about twenty-two feet—but the watchman was unconvinced. "It appeared to me that if he had jumped out of the window pointed out[wards], he would not be lying in the position he was," Shehan explained. Besides, the window was about nine feet to one side.

Shehan hoisted the body onto his back and carried it down the steep slope of George Street to the police station on the waterfront. There, Dr. James Allan made a quick examination and declared the sailor dead. The sketchy facts Shehan had gathered at the scene did not add up. Murphy had told him that

John Gordon, a carpenter rooming at the tavern, had been upstairs in bed when the sailor fell to his death. But Gordon, when questioned separately by Shehan's partner, Power, claimed he had been downstairs in Murphy's room when the sailor died.

There was one way to get to the bottom of things. Murphy, who had accompanied Shehan to the police station, was placed under arrest. The watchmen returned to the Waterloo and rounded up the remaining occupants until a coroner's inquest could determine whether the sailor was the victim of suicide, an accidental fall or murder.

Alexander Allan and several other crewmen of *HMS Cumberland* had rowed ashore about suppertime on September 7 for a night on the town. Allan was about twenty-five and described as "a powerful muscular man" with a head of thick, curly black hair. "He was a very sober, industrious, steady young man" in the estimation of one of his shipmates. Allan, who had been on *Cumberland* for about three years, had sworn off liquor as he neared the end of his tour of duty. Another crewman recollected that he had only seen Allan drunk once in the previous six months. But Allan had a reputation as a scrapper and, drunk or sober, he was usually up for a fight.

The sailors headed straight for "The Hill"—the name given the bars and houses of ill-repute that flourished in the shadow of the ramparts of Halifax's Citadel. "Here gathered an evil slum of grog sellers, pimps, and prostitutes who battened on the dissolute soldiery," Thomas Raddall wrote in *Warden of the North.* There was no shortage of establishments on the waterfront, but Raddall noted that sailors sometimes ventured the half-dozen blocks inland to Barrack Street, where encounters with soldiers often ended in fights. "They never can agree," one seafarer said of soldiers and sailors.

Of course, all this drinking, carousing and fighting did not sit well with Halifax's upper classes. Argyle Street, sandwiched between the waterfront and Barrack Street, boasted the fine homes of some of the city's wealthiest citizens. And the blight was spreading. In an October 1853 letter to the *Novascotian*

93

newspaper, a writer complained that Grafton Street, a block up the hill from Argyle, "has become an abominable den of prostitutes ... and a nuisance and annoyance to the respectable Citizens residing in that neighbourhood."

The first stop for Allan and company was the Waterloo. Murphy had been in business for six years and kept out of trouble with the law by closing on time and barring youths from the premises. Although he claimed he sold "nothing but liquor," officials turned a blind eye to Murphy's profitable sideline —the four prostitutes who plied their trade in the upstairs rooms.

Allan was at the Waterloo between six and seven o'clock and drank only ginger beer. About eight, he met up with another *Cumberland* crewman, Anthony Bainbridge, at Mitty Johnson's Tavern, but cleared out after a scuffle with a group of soldiers wielding sticks. Allan then went looking for his former girlfriend, Margaret Murphy.

Described by one tavernkeeper as a "common prostitute" and "a woman addicted to drinking," she was the estranged wife of the owner of the Waterloo Tavern. Margaret and Thomas Murphy had been separated for about five years, and during the summer of 1852 she and Allan had lived together. The liaison had caused bitterness between Allan and Thomas Murphy. "Murphy seemed to have a spite against him," noted one sailor. Murphy had refused to serve Allan and had once thrown him out of the Waterloo, uttering vague threats to "give him what he had promised him a long time ago "

Allan was no longer living with Margaret Murphy by the summer of 1853, but he was outraged to find her at Young's Tavern in the company of one of his shipmates, Peter Lawrie. Allan called Lawrie into the street but got the worst of the fight and ended up lying in a gutter, bleeding from a small cut above one eye. After passersby helped him to his feet, Allan shook hands with Lawrie, who insisted they "parted friends." Margaret Murphy stayed with Lawrie, and Allan, who seemed to have a nose for trouble, headed back to the Waterloo.

He arrived shortly after eleven. There were two versions of what happened inside the tavern, one told by a sailor and the other by Thomas Murphy and his compatriots. William Giles of *Cumberland* later testified that a fiddler was playing and he and Allan danced with two of the women, then treated them to a drink at the bar. When Allan gave a glass of brandy to Murphy's housekeeper, Mary Ann Cole, Giles said the following exchange took place: "Murphy asked her [Cole] what she took it for when she could get plenty; Allan then asked Murphy what he was looking at him for, and if he owed him anything—if so, he was able to pay him. Murphy told him to clear out, or by God he would give him what he had promised him that six weeks past." Allan, ever the diplomat, ended the conversation by pointing out that Cole was "only a whore."

But Giles's story did not stack up in one respect—he insisted there was no blood on Allan's face. Several independent witnesses said blood could be seen coming from the wound Allan suffered earlier in the street fight.

Murphy's account is even more suspicious. He denied even knowing Allan's name prior to the sailor's arrival at the Waterloo on September 7. Murphy said he was just about to close for the night when Allan entered about quarter past eleven and had a drink at the bar. His face was bleeding badly and he seemed "confused in his mind." Murphy suggested he go upstairs and have one of the women wash off the blood. "The last words he spoke to me were, 'Tom, I am sorry to have been used this way by my shipmates.'" Murphy swore he was writing in his room about thirty minutes later when he heard glass break and found Allan lying dead on the stairs.

The other occupants of the tavern—Cole; two other prostitutes named Matilda Ballard and Sarah Myers; a servant, David Parsons; and the boarder, Gordon—told similar stories at the coroner's inquest convened the day after the death. But the doctor who examined the body testified there was "no doubt" Allan's death "was caused by violence" rather than by a fall. The coroner's jury, composed of six sailors and six civilians in the interest of fairness, returned a verdict charging Murphy, Gordon, Cole, Parsons, Ballard, and Myers with murder. The six were jailed pending trial.

Allan's death strained relations between the military men stationed in Halifax and their civilian hosts. City officials, fearing sailors from *Cumberland* would seek revenge by trashing the Waterloo, swore in one hundred special constables on September 8, the day after Allan was killed. The local military commander agreed to cancel shore leave to help defuse the situation.

The incident also brought Haligonians face-to-face with the seamy underside of life in their city. "Why are these fearful dens of iniquity suffered to exist?" asked the *British Colonist*. "It is believed that many a murder is committed in them. Occasionally on the clearing out of a well, or after a fire, a body has been found. Why do not the Aldermen make a clean sweep, and clear out the wretches who turn our city into a Gomorrah? ... If the house of Murphy is allowed again to be tenanted by a brothel keeper," the newspaper warned, "it will be a vile disgrace."

Meanwhile, cracks began appearing in the united front put up by the six accused. James Wilson, the city jailor, knew Cole and spoke to her briefly before she was locked up. "Mary, has it come to this?" he asked. "I had nothing to do with it," she replied, bursting into tears. "I was in Tom's room when they were upstairs killing the man." Cole would say no more and later denied making the statement.

During the fall of 1853 Joseph Howe, the provincial secretary, visited the jail. It was an official visit, prompted by complaints that the facility was not secure. Howe, regarded as the champion of a free press and one of the architects of responsible government, proved he was also adept at cracking a murder case. The jailor introduced Howe to Myers and Ballard during the tour. Weeks later, they asked to see the famous politician. Myers explained that she did not know Howe but she "thought he was the fittest man" to hear what she and Ballard had to say. Howe maintained he "said nothing to induce the confession made by the girls; I made them no promise." But he did admit he "went to the extent of assuring the girls that in the event of their telling all they knew they would be protected by the government from injury."

Joseph Howe's routine inspection of the Halifax prison provided the confessions that put four people on trial for the murder of a Royal Navy sailor. (*Chronicle-Herald/Mail-Star* files)

Myers, twenty-three, and Ballard, nineteen, told a similar story. Myers took Allan upstairs to her room to wash his face at a basin, then returned to the bar, where she was talking with Ballard and Parsons when they heard a noise upstairs. Ballard said it sounded like "shuffling feet." Then Myers described a cry "as if a man was struck over the head by someone."

The women and Parsons went to the door leading to the street and saw Murphy and Gordon dragging Allan down the stairs. Gordon had him by the waist, Murphy held him by the throat. "He [Allan] was not struggling—he seemed to be pretty well gone," said Myers. Ballard, however, swore that the sailor continued to screech as he was carried outside. Then Gordon struck Allan on the head with something—neither woman could tell what—and returned inside.

When Murphy entered, his hands were covered with blood. He ordered the women to their rooms and warned "if you say a word about this I will take your life as I did that of the sailor." Fearful that Murphy would make good on his threat, Ballard and Myers said they had lied at the coroner's inquest.

The Crown dropped charges against the two women in return for their testimony at the upcoming trial. Their stay in prison improved markedly in the wake of their confession, and Myers was even paid ten shillings a month to work in the jailor's kitchen. At trial, defence lawyers would hint that such treatment was a strong motive to lie about how Allan had died.

Four people remained accused of causing Allan's death. A grand jury reviewed the evidence, including the confessions, later in the fall of 1853 and ordered Murphy and Gordon to stand trial for murder. The charge against Parsons and Cole was reduced to being an accessory after the fact to murder for harbouring the other two after the crime was committed.

The trial opened before the Supreme Court on April 21, 1854. The presiding judge was Thomas Chandler Haliburton, whose literary creation, the fast-talking Yankee pedlar Sam Slick, had already made him a internationally known satirist. "As a judge, Haliburton was conscientious, upright, intelligent, adhering to the spirit rather than to the letter of the law," wrote one biographer. "He was, however, in no sense a great judge, and his propensity for punning and his strong sense of the ludicrous, although often enlivening an otherwise dull courtroom session, did not add to his reputation."

The circumstances of Allan's death and the dubious credentials of the parties involved ensured this trial would be anything but dull. In his opening address to the jury, William Young, a diminutive Scotsman who had assumed the posts of premier and attorney general earlier in the month, cautioned that "this trial will reveal a scene from which, it is true, few communities like this are exempt—but which, when brought distinctly and vividly before us, pain and shock the moral sense of every right-thinking man." Young also candidly admitted that his case rested on the word of two prostitutes, women whose character "may not be all we could wish."

The trial lasted three days. Dr. Allan, who first examined the body, attributed the case of death to a massive fracture extending from the top of the head to the base of the skull. "It must have been caused by some heavy and tremendous blow," he testified, probably inflicted with a flat instrument. In his opinion, "a man jumping out of window in question could not have sustained those injuries." The defence, led by future premier James W. Johnston, tried without success to suggest that the sailor could have received the injury in a fall. Even Haliburton tested the doctor's testimony, asking if a man could receive such an injury in a fall and move nine feet—the distance Allan was lying to the side of the window—before dying. "It was possible," replied Dr. Allan, "but not at all probable."

The next noteworthy witness was Richard Powell, a Hants County farmer who had been in Halifax on September 7 to sell a load of produce. As he walked along Barrack Street about midnight, he testified, two men emerged from the door of the Waterloo Tavern and threw another man down the stairs. Then he claimed he heard the cry of "Murder." Powell said he did not come forward at the coroner's inquest because "I wanted to keep out of trouble," but he had subsequently been subpoenaed by the Crown and given a one-pound note to cover his expenses to appear at the trial. Johnston, regarded as one of the best public speakers of his time, made short work of Powell on cross-examination. After establishing that Powell was an habitual drinker ("I take a horn of grog whenever I can catch it," he admitted), Johnston deftly poked holes in his testimony. Powell responded by being evasive and making jokes, twice drawing rebukes from the bench. By the time the defence lawyer was finished, Powell's evidence was useless.

Myers and Ballard appeared before the jury and repeated their statements implicating Murphy and his cohorts. Myers stood up well under defence questioning, but one newspaper reporter noted that Ballard seemed confused during Johnston's lengthy and detailed cross-examination. After calling Howe to outline the circumstances of the confessions, Young rested the Crown's case.

The defence opened by seeking a directed verdict of not guilty for Cole and Parsons because of the lack of evidence they acted as accessories. Haliburton granted the request, and the two were released from custody. In those days people accused of crimes could not testify; now Cole and Parsons were free to take the witness stand for the remaining defendants, Murphy and Gordon.

The evidence of John Patterson, the first defence witness, created a sensation in the court. After fishing on the North West Arm, he returned to the city about midnight on September 7 and saw a man hanging by his hands from a window ledge of the Waterloo Tavern. The man fell to the stairs, and someone came out the front door, said "Good God, I believe the man is dead," and ran off after a watchman. Patterson, who lived in the small Halifax County community of Terence Bay, said he had never been inside the Waterloo and did not know either Murphy or Gordon.

The prosecutor questioned why Patterson had not come forward earlier. "I did not tell at the outset because the girls first told the right story, that the man had fallen from the window," Patterson replied, standing his ground. "I only came forward when I heard they had contradicted their own testimony and sworn that Gordon and Murphy murdered the man .... Any one who swears that this was the case lies."

Parsons took the stand and denied he, Myers and Ballard had seen Murphy and Gordon carry Allan down the stairs. "The whole story of Ballard and Myers is a lie from beginning to end," he claimed. Parsons, Gordon and Murphy had found Allan's body lying on the stairs, he testified, and Murphy ran for the watchmen.

Haliburton had heard enough. He took the unusual step of interrupting the trial and went into a huddle at the front of the courtroom with the attorney general and Chief Justice Brenton Halliburton and Mr. Justice William Blowers Bliss, two other judges who were on the bench as spectators. Young returned to his place and the trial judge, Haliburton, repeated their discussions for the record. In light of the "very contradictory testimony," he said, "I am sure no jury would feel themselves justified in convicting the prisoners." Young agreed that the Crown's evidence, already "clouded with suspicion" because of the profession of his two chief witnesses, had been crippled by the contradictory evidence of Patterson and Parsons. "I think the case should here conclude," he said.

Chief Justice Halliburton, no relation to the trial judge despite their similar surnames, broke in. "What I feel is this, that in a capital case, where the lives of the parties arraigned are at stake upon testimony so contradictory and conflicting, no jury could feel themselves at liberty, and no Judge would be authorized under such circumstances in instructing them to convict." Having judges sitting in as spectators had its advantages; Bliss concurred, in effect giving the appeal court's stamp of approval on the spot.

Mr. Justice Haliburton asked the jurors to stand. "Whether the unfortunate man Allan met his death by some act of folly or madness of his own or whether his life was taken by the prisoners at the bar or by any other persons is enveloped in mystery—so entire and so complete that human judgement is baffled," he explained. "I have therefore to recommend gentlemen that you return a verdict of not guilty." The jurors held a brief discussion without leaving the jury box and acquitted Murphy and Gordon.

The judge was not about to let the two men completely off the hook. Their escape had been "a fortunate one," Haliburton reminded the pair, based on "the Providential production of certain counter-testimony." Then he launched into a lecture. Gordon, a man able to support himself with a trade, had chosen to live in a bawdy house "as a bully or a partner." Murphy had degraded himself "below the dignity of manhood to engage in the occupation almost of a beast." He admonished both men to seek an honest calling and chided Halifax authorities for granting licences for the sale of liquor in brothels like the Waterloo.

How Alexander Allan met his death remains shrouded in a web of lies and accusations. The evils of Barrack Street, thrown into stark relief by the trial, persisted for at least another decade. In 1870, the *Morning Chronicle* reported, the area still featured "scenes of drunkenness and riot requiring the largest part of the policeman's time." But the military issued an order in May of that year banning sailors and soldiers from the Barrack Street area; taverns and brothels, robbed of their clientele, closed or moved to other parts of the city.

As for the Waterloo Tavern, it was eventually torn down and replaced with a brick building devoted to more exalted pursuits as the site of the Salvation Army Citadel. And the street itself was given a new name—Brunswick Street—to help erase the stigma of the past. But history has a habit of repeating itself. In the 1980s, the site of the Waterloo Tavern became the home of one of Halifax's first late-night cabarets.

Chapter 9

―――――――――――――――――――――――――――――――――――

Black day at the polls

TO THE POLLS, MEN! TO THE POLLS! Go at it today, in right good earnest. Go at it in right good humour. Spare no effort to win. Do to those opposed to you as you would be done by. Maintain your rights. But do so peaceably. Give no offence. Take no offence. Take, but give no insults. Poll your votes. Poll them *every* one. Give no cause of provocation. Act like men who know what their rights are, and know how to maintain them. Be *sober*, be vigilant.

Morning Chronicle, Halifax, May 12, 1859.

Passions were running high as hundreds of men descended on the tiny community of Grand Lake on May 12, 1859, to cast their ballots. This was no ordinary election—it was a fight for political supremacy between Catholic and Protestant. And in the midst of fields and farms clustered on the shore of Grand Lake, some fifteen miles north of Halifax, the struggle was about to erupt into open warfare.

All morning, men had been filing in and out of the polling station. Across the road at White's Hotel, the upstairs had been rented by the opposing parties to refresh their troops. Liberals quaffed ale, ate and talked politics in one room; next door, the hated Tories did the same. There was no shortage of men eager to pick a fight. Patrick Hurley and Bryan Kennedy, two burly Irish railway workers, led a group of Tories who shoved their way into the Liberals' room. One man was struck in the face with a

103

IMPORTANT DISCOVERY !!!

Hole and Corner Bigotry Exposed. Know Nothing Conspiracy in Halifax against 80 Thousand of the Queen's Subjects Detected!

This Day is Published, Price One Penny,

THE SECRET CIRCULAR OF THE (so called) "PROTESTANT ALLIANCE,"

In which the most atrocious Sentiments are avowed; the most insulting Language used; and a ferocious Persecution Declared—against ONE THIRD of Her Majesty's Subjects in Nova Scotia; and ONE HALF of the Citizens of Halifax, by a few Cowardly Plotters, whose Deeds of Darkness are now Dragged Forth into the Light of Day.

TOGETHER WITH THE NAMES OF THIS BAND OF BIGOTS, COPIED FROM THEIR OWN CIRCULAR.

The Copy of the Circular from which this Publication is printed, is one which was Franked by Benjamin Wier, M.P.P. And is the First Fruits of the Wicked Manifesto Publicly Endorsed and Sanctioned on the 5th Day of March, 1857, in their places in the House of Assembly, by WILLIAM YOUNG, JOSEPH HOWE, BENJAMIN WIER, WILLIAM ANNAND & CO.

Friends of Civil and Religious Liberty : : :

CIRCULATE THIS DOCUMENT THRO' THE LENGTH & BREADTH OF NOVA SCOTIA!

That all Honest Men and True Christians may UNITE in Crushing the Hydra of Bigotry, and Maintaining the Fair Fame of our fine Province; in which every Man is permitted to Worship his God according to his Conscience, without Pains, Penalties, or Disabilities.

GOD SAVE THE QUEEN.

Part of a Catholic handbill criticizing the Protestant Alliance that circulated prior to the 1859 Nova Scotia election. Sectarian tensions were at the boiling point when voters descended on the Grand Lake polling station. (Public Archives of Nova Scotia/Manuscript collection) tumbler and cut before James White, the hotelkeeper, stepped in and ordered the Tories out.

Outside, more trouble was brewing. Whenever Tories and Liberals crossed paths, threats or insults were exchanged. Minor scuffles broke out. At one point, George Preeper and George Gray were leaning out a second-storey window of the hotel as Hurley and another man, John Carroll, walked below. "Draw in your head, you Protestant son of a bitch," Hurley shouted. "You damn Catholic son of a bitch," Gray shot back, shaking his fist. That did it. When Gray came out of the hotel a few minutes later, he was jumped and beaten by a gang of Tories. When another Liberal, Thomas Lowrie, tried to intervene, the attackers turned on him.

About a dozen Liberals decided enough was enough. They ran up the road to the farm of James Kenty, where rifles and shotguns had been stashed earlier in the day. Heading back to White's Hotel to save their comrades, they were met by upwards of a hundred Tories, some wielding sticks and rocks. "The two parties were in an attitude of war," noted a man who ran for cover.

"Stay back," shouted one of the armed men. Another fired a shot into the air but the Tories, emboldened by liquor and their superior numbers, kept advancing. They overran the Liberals, grabbing guns and breaking them. Some Liberals were beaten with the stocks of their own guns; the rest retreated a few yards and turned to make a second stand. Hurley lunged for Preeper's gun. Preeper scrambled onto a pile of logs and raised his double-barrelled shotgun to his shoulder. Hurley was still coming at him as Preeper fired. Hurley collapsed, blood pouring from a gaping wound to his neck. He bled to death within minutes.

Preeper ran through a brook and fled into the woods. The Tories, seeing one of their number dead, savagely beat the handful of Liberals who were unable to escape, including the party's chief scrutineer, who had remained at the polling booth and took no part in the riot. Miraculously, Hurley was the only fatality of one of the blackest days in Nova Scotia electoral history.

Violence was not a new element in Nova Scotia elections. Our grandfathers and great-grandfathers took their politics seriously, and if defending the cause meant buying votes or busting the heads of a few opponents on election day, so be it. And the results could be deadly. During the 1830 election a gang of sailors armed with sticks started a riot. One man was killed. But Nova Scotians have yet to witness an election that rivals the bitterness and hatred of the 1859 campaign. The main issue was something that went deeper than railway policy or provincial finances—the rallying cry was religion. "This election," noted Nova Scotia's top political historian, J. Murray Beck, "was the only one in provincial history primarily fought and decided on the religious question." It was a no-holds-barred battle for political power between the province's Protestants and Catholics.

Sectarian tension spilled over into the political arena in the mid-1850s. Acadian and Scottish Catholics were uneasy within the ranks of the Liberal government after Premier William Young, faced with Protestant criticism, withdrew a proposal for separate Catholic schools. When the House of Assembly opened in February 1857, they made their move. Eight Catholic MLAs crossed the floor and Young's government fell on a non-confidence motion. James W. Johnston, the Conservative leader, formed a new administration dependent on Catholic support. In the Liberal press, Johnston was lambasted as a political opportunist controlled by a Catholic minority bent on imposing its will on the Protestant majority.

By the time Johnston went to the polls in the spring of 1859, emotions had been whipped to a fever pitch. Each side blamed the other for starting the strife. The highly partisan press of the day pleaded for order on election day, but in the same breath spread fear and suspicion. The *British Colonist*, the government paper, reported that an opposition politician had advised Liberal supporters to arm themselves. The Liberal's *Novascotian* called that charge "a base, black slander," but warned its readers that "a row, on Election day, is almost certain to lead to a *riot*. A riot in this City [Halifax], just now, might end in a conflagration or other terrible disaster—perhaps the loss of life or some fearful calamity."

It took several days to tally the votes and declare the winners. Telegraph lines between Halifax and several outlying counties were down, leaving the outcome in doubt. Two days after the polls closed the *Colonist* predicted "a decided majority" for the government. It was wishful thinking. The Liberals, riding the Protestant backlash against the government, won a narrow majority, twenty-nine of fifty-five seats. "The Government is beaten. Soundly beaten," the *Novascotian* proclaimed on May 16. "Nova Scotia is herself again .... She has thrown off the yoke of tyranny ... Nova Scotia, Protestant Nova Scotia, is free."

Among the victorious Liberals were John Esson, a merchant, and publisher William Annand, whose newspaper holdings included the *Novascotian* and the *Chronicle*. The pair defeated the government candidates, Falconer and Gladwin, by some seven hundred votes in the eastern division of Halifax County. But their election was overshadowed by Hurley's death and the rioting at Grand Lake. In voting that was cut short by the riot, the Tory candidates took 78 and 79 votes at the poll, compared to 35 and 34 respectively for Esson and Annand.

The *Colonist* described Hurley's shooting as "cold-blooded, premeditated and cruel murder, perpetrated with the view of driving from the polls the friends of Messrs. Falconer and Gladwin." The *Novascotian*, however, accused the government of sparking the violence by bringing in Irish Catholic railway workers to vote for its candidates. The *Acadian Recorder*, pro-Conservative despite its claims of independence, called the incident "the darkest page in the history of such contests that Nova Scotia can produce since this Province has had a House of Assembly."

More shrill rhetoric was to come in the weeks following the election. The Conservatives charged that the opposition had used bribery, intimidation, lies, vote-buying and "every species of rowdyism" to win. The government press also accused Esson and Annand of spreading false rumours that Catholic gangs were about to sack the Grand Lake area to avenge Hurley's death. The Liberals fired back, accusing the government of buying votes through generous gifts of boots, hats, shawls and rum. According to the *Novascotian*, one government supporter, asked if he was planning to vote, replied: "Och, by jappers, and isn't it tired of voting I am?" And the Catholic clergy, it was said, had instructed members of their congregations to vote Conservative or face excommunication.

As the war of words raged in the press, Preeper and nine others were charged with murder. Preeper and two brothers, John and James Kenty, turned themselves in shortly after the shooting and were jailed; the other seven remained at large. The next sitting of the Supreme Court in Halifax was set for the fall of 1859, but Preeper petitioned the lieutenant governor, Lord Mulgrave, in July seeking a special session of the court to hear his case. Preeper pleaded that he was "one of a large family who are unfortunate in having a dissipated Father, and ... had been of late years the chief support of his Mother and [her] six small children." Preeper, claiming his health had been "greatly impaired" by two months behind bars, said he was "entirely innocent" of the charge and he welcomed an early court date to establish his innocence. He marked the petition with an X. The Kenty brothers filed a similar request.

The petitions were passed on to the courts, but Chief Justice Brenton Halliburton had been reading the papers. "As the death of the party took place during an affray at a contested Election," he replied on July 22, "it would be injudicious to hasten the trial, as it is more probable that Justice would be done both to the public and the prisoners if it took place at the usual sittings of the Court in October next, where a longer time would have elapsed for the public mind to cool, after the excitement apt to exist on both sides upon so sad an event." The three men languished in prison for three more months.

The timing of the trial would also determine how strongly the Crown would press for a conviction. Despite their defeat at the polls, the Conservatives were in no hurry to hand over the reins to the Liberals. The party clung to power until the legislature met in January 1860, when it was voted out of office by the Liberal majority in the assembly. In the meantime it was business as usual; James W. Johnston, who was attorney general as well as premier, handled the prosecution. Since the victim, Hurley, had

Defence lawyer Jonathan McCully earned a stern rebuke from the bench when he contended that George Preeper's trial was "political." (*Chronicle-Herald/Mail-Star* files)

been a Conservative supporter, the Crown went all out in its effort to send the accused to the gallows. Had Preeper's party taken office immediately after the election, the trial would undoubtedly have taken a different course.

There was controversy from the moment the case was called on the docket. The first step was to have the charges reviewed by a twenty-four-man grand jury, which would hear evidence and determine if there was enough evidence to send the accused to trial. If the grand jurors found there was enough evidence, they would return a true bill; if not, there would be no bill and the prosecution would cease. Mr. Justice William Blowers Bliss, probably the keenest legal mind on the Supreme Court, instructed the grand jury on October 27, reminding them that "if a number of persons were assembled together, and one committed murder, the others aiding and abetting, all were equally guilty of the crime." The grand jury—only seventeen strong because of no-shows—in due course returned true bills against all ten accused.

But the prosecution ground to a halt when the attorney general moved the arraignment the following week. Defence lawyers William Young, who was poised to reclaim the premier's office, and Jonathan McCully, another prominent Liberal, announced they had proof only nine of the 17 grand jurors had agreed to return the true bills. The law required the agreement of at least a dozen grand jurors for charges to proceed.

Bliss was not on the bench for the legal flap that followed. It was left to Mr. Justice Lewis Morris Wilkins to try to sort out the mess. Grand jury proceedings were supposed to be secret, and some lawyers questioned whether the vote could be revealed in court. Wilkins decided to forge ahead, saying there was nothing he could do. Preeper and the Kenty brothers, still the only three in custody, pleaded "not guilty under protest," and the trial was set to begin the following week.

But Wilkins, who was only in his second year on the bench, took advantage of a recess to run his decision by Halliburton and Bliss. No lack of judicial expertise here—the octogenarian chief justice had been on the bench for an astounding fifty-seven years, Bliss for twenty-five. Wilkins returned to the courtroom and announced that "substantial justice might be defeated altogether ... especially in a case of life and death" unless the jury was resummoned. Grand jurors, he ruled, could disclose an error in their verdict without revealing the substance of their deliberations.

Eight days later, the court reconvened. The grand jurors had been rounded up and foreman William Metzler admitted that the members had voted nine to eight to hand down the murder indictment. Bliss, who accompanied Wilkins to court to sort out the mess, said it would be "a solemn mockery" to proceed with a trial. He ordered the murder indictment quashed. The attorney general promptly submitted a new one charging the same ten men with the lesser offence of manslaughter. The jurors reheard evidence but found a true bill against Preeper only. The Kenty brothers were freed and Preeper's trial was set to begin November 14. If convicted, he faced a fine or a prison term of up to 14 years.

"The case is one necessarily of a political character," contended McCully, a thin-faced man with absurdly long sideburns that dangled from either side of his head. "The whole difficulty arose between two political parties." That was the defence's pitch to the jury when Preeper stepped into the prisoner's dock for trial. It was not simply grandstanding on McCully's part: the case was, indeed, all about politics. The setting was the close quarters of the Supreme Court room in Province House—now home of the legislative library—one door down from the legislative assembly chamber. Tory lawyers were lined up at the prosecution table; Liberal barristers were seated behind them for the defence. And partisanship coloured the testimony of almost every witness.

What happened on election day at the Grand Lake polling station became a tangle of conflicting evidence, and the two stories that emerged were split along political lines. The Crown's dozen witnesses, all but one of whom had voted Tory, painted a picture of docile railway workers suddenly challenged by a group of unruly Liberals armed with guns. They said they had attacked the Liberals to disarm them. The twenty or so witnesses called by the defence—most of whom voted had Liberal—told a different story. The railway workers, they said, had been spoiling

111

for a fight all day, intimidating Liberal voters with insults and threats. When the Liberals fetched their guns to protect themselves, the riot erupted and Preeper killed Hurley in self-defence.

Extracting the truth from those divergent stories presented a formidable task. In retrospect, the events of May 12, 1859 seem closer to the defence version. Consider, for instance, the evidence of Bryan Kennedy, a Crown witness. A Newfoundlander who had been in Nova Scotia for five years, he was employed on the government railway to repair track. Questioned by the attorney general, Kennedy said the Tory supporters marched toward the Liberals and told them to put down their guns. When they refused, the Tories began taking the guns away. Kennedy said he carried a hardwood stick but was the only Tory carrying any kind of weapon. He said nothing about having used it.

Then came McCully's turn. Under cross-examination, Kennedy admitted he had heard there might be trouble and had stashed the stick under White's Hotel earlier in the day. Yes, he conceded, he had used the the stick during the riot, knocking down several Liberals. And yes, he had gone for Preeper but had slipped and fallen before reaching him. Even so, he had managed to give Preeper a glancing blow to the head. This was moments before Hurley was shot. In the wake of the shooting, Kennedy conceded, the Tories went wild. They took revenge on a handful of Liberals who were too badly injured to run away, beating them even more. "Some of our side wanted to kill them," Kennedy told the defence lawyer, "and others wouldn't let them." For his part, Kennedy seized one of the injured men and dragged him by the hair.

Obviously, Kennedy and his colleagues were no angels. Once the defence began presenting evidence, the focus shifted to events leading up to the shooting. Philip Brown, an agent for the Inland Navigation Company, said he dropped by White's Hotel to pick up some of his employees when two railway workers struck him from behind. "These men were going about evidently striving to kick up a row." One of the men asked Brown if he was going to vote. Brown said he wasn't. "In God's name you had better not," the man warned, "for if you do, you had better

112

prepare your coffin." In contrast, Brown testified, the Liberals "behaved in a great orderly manner."

In the wake of the shooting, the Liberal press had charged that the navvies were purposely sent to Grand Lake to disrupt the election. Defence evidence lent credence to that allegation. James Hunt, a conductor on the Nova Scotia Railway, testified his train picked up at least twenty-five railway workers at various stations between Halifax and Grand Lake on the morning of the election. More were brought down from Enfield. All were carried free, Hunt said, by order of a high-ranking railway official. More damning was evidence that the government had paid the railway workers for election day, even though they were given the day off to vote. Other defence witnesses cast doubt on the claim that the navvies were unarmed. Several witnesses said the Tories advanced on the Liberals armed with rocks, sticks and crowbars; some maintained Hurley had rocks in his hands as he lunged at Preeper.

To establish that the Liberals had reason to fear the worst on election day, the defence called John Kenty. Kenty described how three railway workers had come to his house a week before the election and threatened to beat him because he was canvassing for the Liberals. Kenty was struck across the head before he could escape. On election day, a group of Liberals showed up and asked Kenty, who lived just up the road from White's Hotel, to store their guns in case there was trouble. Kenty let them put the guns, hidden in rolled-up rugs and quilts, in a spare room. Kenty acted as an inspector for the Liberal candidates at the polls, but was threatened by the navvies. "I was frightened for my life," he said, and fled, with his wife and children in tow, moments before the shooting started.

The biggest obstacle for the defence was the man surveying the courtroom from the bench. Wilkins, a tough and opinionated judge, had been appointed by the Liberals in 1856, but he came down hard on McCully and Young, who were former cabinet colleagues. He was either trying to prevent any appearance of favouritism or had abandoned his partisanship when he assumed judicial office. If the latter were true, Wilkins was one of the few judges of the time to leave his political views at the courtroom door. Then again, Wilkins might have been having trouble deciding which party he favoured. He had started his political career as a Conservative, jumped to the Liberals, then returned to the Tory fold, only to switch to the Liberals in return for the judgeship he had long coveted.

During Kenty's testimony, Wilkins interrupted when he felt the witness was straying too far from the events of election day. He did not mince words. "I must say that the defence in this case had been conducted in a manner most discreditable to a British Court of Justice," he snapped. McCully and Young protested that they had to show that the Liberals had grounds to bring guns to protect themselves. After a brief, heated argument, Wilkins relented.

More harsh words were to come. Wilkins devoted most of his charge to the twelve-man jury to a scathing attack on McCully's assertion that the trial was a political one. "I will not insult you by the supposition that you could possibly be induced to regard this case as a *political question*, or to permit any other influences to affect your deliberations than grave and matured considerations of duty," he told the jurors. "If you and I could be brought to prostitute our offices in the Temple of Justice to political partisanship ... what security would a Colonial subject have for his property, his liberty, his life?"

The charge was an outright condemnation of Preeper. Wilkins told the jurors to ignore the beatings inflicted on Liberals after the shooting. The Liberals, he contended, were not justified in taking up arms to defend themselves. But for the evidence that Hurley was holding rocks when he lunged at Preeper, the judge said bluntly, Preeper would have been guilty of murder. And there was no question of his guilt on the manslaughter indictment. "I am bound to say, the law and the evidence, *in any view of the facts in proof*," Wilkins emphasized, "constrain you to find him guilty."

Whether the jury would heed the judge's order to convict was another question. The Tory press later charged that the bulk of the jurors were Liberal supporters; the foreman, Charles Tropolet, was described as "perhaps the most inveterate radical"—read die-hard Liberal—in Halifax.

The jurors' sympathy for Preeper became obvious as the judge began reviewing the testimony. "Gentlemen," Wilkins said, looking up from his notes, "I perceive from the listlessness and indifference which some of you are exhibiting that I am performing ... a useless labor. I am reading over these long notes, not for my amusement, but for your information. Be so good," he added, his voice dripping with sarcasm, "as to tell me whether you wish me to proceed?"

There was a long pause. "I believe the jury feel that they already know enough of the case," replied Tropolet, proving himself one of the most brazen foremen ever to head a jury. Wilkins snapped shut his notebook. "I have the honour to sit here as a British Judge," he began, barely containing his anger. "I have a deep sense of the obligations which attach to that office. I have endeavoured, in this exciting and important cause, to discharge them truly and correctly .... *My* duties and responsibilities in this matter are ended. *Yours* now commence."

The jurors retired for barely half an hour before returning a verdict of not guilty. But feelings whipped up by the election and trial remained near the boiling point. "Murder him," someone shouted from the public gallery moments after the verdict was announced. Preeper, for his own safety, had to be spirited out of Province House by sheriff's constables.

The jurors had to ignore a lot of evidence to reach their verdict. There was no question that Preeper had fired the shot that killed Hurley; that was probably the only point on which Liberals and Conservatives agreed. And using a gun to kill a man armed only with rocks did not fit the legal definition of self-defence. Preeper's best plea was that he was provoked to shoot, and in the eyes of the law that still made him guilty of manslaughter. But should Preeper alone have been punished for his role in a riot instigated by men who were being let off scot-free? Even a non-partisan jury could be excused for ignoring the letter of the law in the circumstances.

"The verdict rendered will meet with a hearty response throughout the length and breadth of the land," the *Chronicle* predicted. That was the Liberal view. The Tory *British Colonist* termed the outcome a "whitewash." Charges and counter-charges flew in the press for weeks after the trial. The *Chronicle* accused the attorney general's son of trying to counsel a witness to commit perjury. In the *Colonist*, Preeper's acquittal was attributed to a "corrupt" grand jury and "a no less accommodating" trial jury. "They will long be remembered as men ... who have shewn that any crime may be perpetrated with impunity provided party interests are at stake."

The man at the centre of the political storm was free for the first time in seven months. George Preeper lived out his life on the Guysborough Road, not far from Grand Lake, earning a reputation as an experienced hunting guide. "There are few sportsmen in the city who have not been to Preeper's shooting or fishing," the Halifax *Evening Mail* noted almost four decades after the trial. "The Guysborough Road has the chief woodcock and partridge covers of the county, and not far from Preeper's are trout lakes, out of which you are sure to get a fare."

Long after his own neck had been on the line, Preeper was involved in another murder trial, this time as a witness. In 1888 he testified on behalf of his nephew, William, who was charged with murdering a farmer he worked for in nearby Meaghers Grant. The alleged motive was the farmer's wife, who was pregnant with William Preeper's child. He was convicted after a sensational trial but the death sentence was commuted to a prison term.

George Preeper enjoyed a final fling in the public spotlight in the summer of 1895. The occasion was his marriage to a twenty-two-year-old black woman named Johnson. The event made news not because of the bride's race, nor the fact that Preeper was old enough to be her grandfather: It was generally assumed he was already married. But, as one reporter put it, Preeper convinced a minister that "the woman with whom he had lived for years, and whom he had introduced as his wife, was no relation to him." Almost forty years after he was cleared of killing a man largely because he had backed the right political party, Preeper managed to beat a bigamy rap.

A bloody feud

Armed with an arrest warrant, Benjamin Elms, a constable for the County of Antigonish, saddled his horse and rode off in search of James Bowie. His best bet was the teenager's father. Just as he suspected, he found Francis Bowie about ten in the morning on the marsh near Tracadie, a village of about two hundred located at the eastern end of the county. Bowie, glowering with disapproval, was watching as his neighbour, Ronald McDonald, and McDonald's wife cut hay.

Both Bowie and McDonald claimed ownership of the land, and every year the dispute flared up when haying season rolled around. But in the summer of 1883, the quarrel between the farmers had taken an ugly turn. In late July, Bowie's son James had threatened to shoot McDonald. On July 31, a few days later, Elms had been dispatched to bring the youth to court.

"You better not have anything to do with this affair," Frank Bowie warned as the constable dismounted.

"I have nothing to do with it, but I have a writ for your son."

"My son has not been seen this week, and you will not see him today."

Elms decided to try to play peacemaker. "It is a pity Ronald McDonald and you don't settle this affair between you."

"I have made him several offers to settle it."

"Would you settle it now, Frank?"

"I would settle it any time."

Elms and Bowie were standing about thirty yards from where the McDonalds were going about their work. Suddenly,

the crack of a gunshot shattered the morning air. Ronald Mc-
Donald fell with a wound to his lower body. Elms, looking for the
source of the shot, saw smoke rising from a nearby clump of
rosebushes. Then James Bowie brazenly stood up from behind a
bush, a rifle in his left hand. Elms began to sprint towards him.

"You need not run after him, you won't catch him," Frank
Bowie shouted. Elms, who was unarmed, heeded the advice, no
doubt confident he could deal with James Bowie later. He
changed direction and ran to help McDonald, who was screaming in agony. James Bowie stood in the bushes and stared as if
admiring his handiwork as his father launched into a tirade.

"Ronald McDonald had been warned time after time not to
come here or else he would be shot. Damn him, he has got it
now." The elder Bowie then turned his invective on McDonald's
wife as she bent over her dying husband. "You damned old
robbing strumpet, you ought to have it just as much."

Elms picked up McDonald and carried him to his house.
Glancing over his shoulder, he saw James Bowie coolly shoulder
his rifle and walk off towards his home, his father close behind.
When Elms reached the McDonald farm, he deposited the
wounded man in a bed and ran for a priest. Annabella Coté, a
friend of the family, helped comfort McDonald. He told the
woman he was dying and took her hand. "The Bowies fixed me
at last," he said. By the time Elms returned, McDonald was dead.
A bitter feud had ended in cold-blooded murder.

The object of the bad blood between the Bowies and the
McDonalds was eight acres of marsh that yielded nothing more
valuable than a cut of hay. McDonald's first wife was Frank
Bowie's sister, and it was through marriage that McDonald
staked his claim to the land. Bowie, an Acadian, got along with
his Scottish neighbour and brother-in-law until his sister died.
McDonald remarried, and Bowie insisted the land had been his
all along. In the fall of 1881, an unseen gunman took a shot at
McDonald, knocking his pipe out of his mouth but causing no
injury. Few doubted it was the work of the Bowies.

Tensions reached the boiling point two years later. Frank
Bowie, who was in his mid-sixties, now had a young ally to help

carry on the feud. James Bowie, one of his seven children, was a sandy-haired, blue-eyed seventeen-year-old, about five-foot nine and ready for trouble. "He bears the reputation of being a lawless young rowdy," noted one newspaper account.

James Bowie jumped into the fray in late July, 1883. William Pettipas, a neighbour, recalled that McDonald asked Pettipas to accompany him to the disputed land. McDonald was obviously hesitant to work the property alone after the ambush. As McDonald cut hay, Pettipas sat on a fence. On the other side, Frank Bowie was hoeing potatoes. Within a few minutes, James Bowie walked up carrying a gun and shouted at his uncle.

"James told Ronald McDonald 'he would shoot him or murder him if he did not keep away from that place,'" said Pettipas. Frank Bowie immediately stepped in, telling his son to "come away from him today and we will fix him another time." James Bowie heeded his father's wishes and retreated. Based on that run-in, an arrest warrant was issued charging James Bowie with threatening McDonald's life. Five days later, before Constable Elms could execute the warrant, the younger Bowie had made good on his threat.

No concerted effort was made to find James Bowie until the evening of July 31, almost eight hours after he gunned down McDonald. About suppertime Elms and two other men descended on the Bowie farm asking for James Bowie. Frank Bowie said his son by that time had probably reached Canso, a fishing community far to the south. Elms walked to a window and began to tell Frank Bowie that McDonald was dead, but stopped in mid-sentence; from his vantage point he saw James Bowie fleeing north across Tracadie Harbour in a small boat. By the time Elms and his companions commandeered a boat to give chase, Bowie had reached Tracadie Big Island, at the mouth of the harbour, and disappeared into the woods.

A party of about twenty men searched the island the following day without success. County Sheriff Henry P. Hill took charge of the case, ordering an autopsy on McDonald's body and directing Elms to arrest Frank Bowie on suspicion of being a party to the murder. Frank Bowie was taken into custody on

August 2, protesting to Elms that he "would not have had McDonald shot in the body for the world." The elder Bowie was lodged in a jail cell in Antigonish, the county seat located about twenty-five miles to the west, to await a court hearing.

Meanwhile, further steps were taken to catch the man who actually pulled the trigger. Sheriff Hill organized a party of fifty men who left Antigonish on a special train on August 5 to comb the island. No trace of the fugitive was found, and the search was called off by mid-afternoon. "The nature of the ground [was] especially favourable to the concealment of a criminal," the sheriff reported to the provincial government the following day. "I am now at a loss what to do ...." James Bowie had apparently made it back to the mainland and his whereabouts were anybody's guess. As a last resort, the sheriff distributed two hundred wanted posters bearing a description of James Bowie and offering a $150 reward for his capture.

With James Bowie at large, the authorities turned their attention to prosecuting his father for his role in the killing. After a preliminary hearing held August 9, Frank Bowie was ordered to stand trial before the Supreme Court on a charge of inciting his son to commit murder. The case went to trial at the court's October sitting in Antigonish, Mr. Justice Robert L. Weatherbe presiding. The Crown established the bitter feeling that had existed between the Bowies and the McDonalds over the patch of land, and the testimony of Elms, the local constable, left no doubt that James Bowie was guilty of murder.

Frank Bowie's guilt was less clear. "There was no direct positive evidence connecting the father and son in such a way as to clearly criminate the father," the Halifax *Morning Herald* reported. "Extremely strong circumstances pointed to a conspiracy upon his part ... [but] some witnesses called by the prosecution were of doubtful reputation, and their evidence in some particulars seemed somewhat colored."

William Pettipas drove the final nail in the Crown's coffin. Pettipas had witnessed the confrontation a few days before the killing and heard Frank Bowie tell his son "we will fix him another time." He was the prosecution's star witness, but he fled the courthouse during a recess without taking the stand. Pettipas, the *Herald*'s reporter contended, "carried away a missing link of in the chain of testimony, which would, it is believed, have altered the verdict." The jury deliberated one hour before finding Frank Bowie not guilty.

Round one went to the defence. The Crown laid a new charge against Bowie as a principal in the second degree to murder and a second trial was convened in June 1884. Under the law of the day, a principal in the second degree was someone who was present when an offence was committed and helped the perpetrator carry out the act. "The fact that a person is actually present at the commission of a crime does not necessarily make him an aider or abettor," explained an 1882 Canadian legal text. "It should be proved that he did or said something showing his consent to the felonious purpose, and contributing to its execution."

The Crown had been unable to prove that Frank Bowie had incited his son to commit murder, but there was evidence he had known about the ambush. Bowie's ravings as McDonald lay wounded showed spite, not surprise. And he had taken steps that had helped his son kill McDonald. He had told Elms his son was not in the area and motioned the constable aside to talk moments before the shooting, as if to keep him out of harm's way when the shot was fired.

The charge was not the only strike against Bowie at his second trial. Pettipas had been rounded up and testified about the run-in between McDonald and the Bowies shortly before the murder. With a new jury, new evidence, and a new charge, the elder Bowie was convicted. "The feeling here is very strongly against the prisoner," noted a press dispatch from Antigonish.

Defence lawyer D.C. Fraser launched an appeal. At the second trial, the defence had pleaded *autrefois acquit*—a time-honoured legal maxim that no one who has been acquitted of a crime can be tried again for that same crime. But Chief Justice James McDonald, the judge at the second trial, ruled that the offence charged in the fall of 1883 was not the same as the offence alleged in the spring of 1884. The full bench of the Supreme

Court—appeals were decided by panels of trial judges until a distinct appeal court was established in Nova Scotia in 1966—agreed and rejected Bowie's appeal. On October 16, Bowie was sentenced to hang on January 8, 1885, for his role in the murder of Ronald McDonald.

Efforts to spare Bowie from the gallows began within weeks. On November 1, Fraser wrote to Senator Alexander Campbell, the justice minister in the federal Conservative government, asking that the death sentence be commuted to a prison term. The lawyer enclosed petitions signed by 194 residents of Tracadie and surrounding communities—clergymen, prominent merchants, politicians, and justices of the peace—asking for clemency for Bowie. The petitioners pointed to Bowie's advanced age and claimed that "public feeling was deeply aroused" but the murder "and the escape of the son caused this feeling to be wholly directed against the father."

In a confidential letter to another federal cabinet minister, Hector Langevin, Fraser charged that prejudice had denied his client a fair trial. Langevin, the minister of public works, was the leading French Canadian in the government, and Fraser pleaded with him to "help a poor countryman condemned to death through popular prejudice rather than upon evidence." To hear Fraser tell it, Bowie had been convicted solely because he was French.

Antigonish County was populated by a mixture of Acadians, Loyalists, and Highland Scots, divided by language but bound together by the dominant religion of the area, Catholicism. Fraser maintained that the Scots, the largest ethnic group in the county, were out to get Bowie for murdering one of their own. "I defended him throughout and feel confident that the jury made up their minds, before hearing a word of evidence, to hang him," he told Langevin. "The murdered man was a Highlander and the whole County was unduly excited about the murder.... I got him [Bowie] off the first time, and this enraged them."

Fraser, a Liberal, took pains to point out that he was not expecting favours from the Tories. "Being politically opposed to your government no one can say my plea is on any ground but

122

what I consider right." He appealed to Langevin "to do what you can" for Bowie. "He is poor and friendless."

The defence lawyer's allegations did not stack up with the facts. If the Scots were out to get Bowie, why had he been acquitted the first time around? True, the jury that convicted Bowie was composed mainly of Scots—three McDonalds, two McLeans, a McAdam, a McKenzie, and a McKinnon accounted for eight of the twelve jurors. But they were far from eager to see Bowie hang. Eleven jurors signed a petition on October 20, 1884, asking the governor general to commute the death sentence. Other petitions sent to Ottawa belie any English-French split over the case. Of the close to two hundred other people who signed petitions on Bowie's behalf, more than one in three bore an English surname.

The weight the government gave to Fraser's dubious contentions is impossible to gauge, and Justice Department records reveal no evidence of intervention by Langevin. But on December 2, barely a month before the date set for execution, cabinet commuted Bowie's sentence to imprisonment for life. Shortly before Christmas 1884, the sixty-five-year-old Bowie was shipped to New Brunswick to live out his remaining days within the fortress-like walls of Dorchester Penitentiary.

Four years later, Bowie's cause had a new champion. John S.D. Thompson, the former Nova Scotia premier and judge who succeeded Campbell as justice minister in 1885, reopened the case the fall of 1888. Thompson's motives are unclear. On one hand, the MP for Antigonish was helping out a constituent; on the other, he was correcting what he perceived to be an injustice. Thompson felt there were serious shortcomings in the evidence of Bowie's guilt.

The man who would later attain the post of prime minister outlined his reservations in a detailed memorandum prepared for cabinet on October 3, 1888. The evidence against Bowie, he argued, "seems ... insufficient to warrant a conviction." The only evidence indicating any complicity in the murder was Bowie's abusive statements after McDonald was shot, and Thompson felt they were understandable given the bitterness of the ongoing

123

land dispute. The run-in witnessed by Pettitpas, in which Bowie told his son they would "fix him [McDonald] another time," could also be explained. Bowie's words "may have been an attempt to interfere with the shooting which otherwise would have taken place at once, or an attempt to put off the son from his design until his passion would subside."

Thompson was willing to stretch the facts to their breaking point to be fair to Bowie. When arrested, Bowie maintained he "would not have had McDonald shot in the body for the world." This statement, said Thompson, showed Bowie thought McDonald had received a less serious wound to the legs and "somewhat extenuated" his harsh words immediately after the shooting. Thompson conveniently overlooked the more likely interpretation: Bowie wanted to see McDonald shot, but not in the body where a fatal wound was more likely.

Thompson had other misgivings about the evidence. The Crown's main witnesses, Pettipas and Elms, were of "questionable reliability," he said. He gave no reason for that assessment, but he felt it was worth mentioning that Elms was black. The justice minister, who had reviewed his department's file on the case, accepted without question defence lawyer Fraser's contention that Bowie's conviction arose "partly from sympathies of race, and partly on account of the successful escape of the son."

"The prisoner has suffered imprisonment for nearly four years which perhaps is not to be regretted considering the bad feeling which existed, and in which he participated," Thompson concluded. Given the "doubtful testimony" that supported the conviction, Bowie's age, his "exemplary" conduct in prison, and time already served, the minister asked that he be released. Five days later, cabinet accepted Thompson's report. Bowie emerged from Dorchester on October 15, 1888, a free man at age sixty-nine.

While Frank Bowie paid his debt to society, his son remained at large. Wanted posters and a reward netted no leads, and it was believed James Bowie had fled to the United States. In the summer of 1887, some Antigonish County natives who had moved to Boston spotted a man they believed to be fugitive. The object of

Halifax police detective Nicholas Power was dispatched to Boston to arrest a man suspected of being the fugitive James Bowie. (Halifax Police Museum)

their suspicions was a young pipefitter named Pitts who lived in the suburb of East Cambridge and worked in Boston. The Nova Scotia authorities were alerted and the East Cambridge police placed Pitts under surveillance.

Nicholas Power, chief detective of the Halifax police, arrived in Boston in November and Pitts was immediately taken into custody. "I am innocent, and am willing to go to Halifax or anywhere else and face the charge," Pitts maintained under questioning at the police station. "I am not the man that is wanted, I can tell you. There is some mistake. I do not know the officer from the Dominion, and I don't think he knows me. Do you, Mr. Officer?" Power, who had had no previous involvement in the case, said he did not.

Pitts admitted he knew of the murder case and had been in the Tracadie area for a visit in 1885. "I stayed around there long enough to be arrested, tried and convicted if I had been guilty. I cannot understand why I am taken in charge by the police for an offence I did not commit." Despite his pleas, Pitts was locked up in the Middlesex County jail to await an extradition hearing. "The Cambridge police say they believe Pitts is innocent," the *Boston Globe* reported. "He appears to be an industrious person."

Power could not identify James Bowie, but Elms was dispatched to Boston to testify at the extradition hearing. It was never held. The Antigonish constable took one look at Pitts and announced they had the wrong man. On November 12, Nova Scotia's attorney general, James W. Longley, received a terse cable from Power: "Prisoner discharged. Not Bowie. Witness [Elms] leaves for home tonight." At the end of 1887, Longley reported that in the six weeks since Pitts was released, "no information has been obtained regarding the whereabouts of Bowie." The trail had again gone cold. James Bowie, Antigonish County's "lawless young rowdy," had made good his escape.

Part Four

Mayhem on the high seas

The folly of Edward Jordan

Three days out of Percé, Quebec, and just off Cape Canso, the captain of the schooner *Three Sisters* went to his cabin to fetch a quadrant to check his position by the noonday sun. "I was standing near the table, directly below the skylight, turning over the leaves of a book," Captain John Stairs recalled of that September day in 1809, "when, looking up I saw Jordan pointing a pistol down the skylight."

Jordan was Edward Jordan, a black-bearded Irishman in his late thirties who had booked passage to Halifax on the vessel with his wife and four young children. In a flash, the startled Stairs ducked as Jordan fired the flintlock through the glass. "The ball grazed my nose and side of my face," said Stairs. But a crewman standing beside him was not so lucky—Thomas Heath was shot in the chest and fell to his knees. "Oh my God," Heath shouted, "I am killed."

Stairs, his face freckled with gunpowder, rifled his cabin for a weapon to defend himself. But his trunk had been forced open and a matched set of pistols taken. His sword, mounted at the head of his berth, was also missing. As he searched, Stairs heard four or five more shots. Rather than wait in his cabin like a sitting duck, he decided to fight it out on deck.

He reached the top of the companionway and came face to face with Jordan, who was brandishing a pistol in one hand and an axe in the other. "I seized his arms and, begging him 'for God's sake, spare my life,' shoved him backwards," said Stairs. In the struggle, Jordan pulled the trigger with a loud snap but the pistol

128

failed to fire. Stairs grabbed the muzzle, wrenched the gun out of Jordan's hand and threw it overboard. Stairs also managed to take the axe. Unable to use it to strike Jordan as they wrestled, he tossed it into the sea as well.

Stairs called for help from the ship's mate, John Kelly, a short, twenty-two-year-old who was standing with his back to the struggle. Kelly made no response. To his horror, Stairs realized Kelly was loading a pistol, and he was Kelly's intended target. "Is it Kelly you want? I'll give you Kelly," shouted Jordan's wife, Margaret, as she hit Stairs on the back with a boat hook. Outnumbered three to one, Stairs broke free from Jordan and headed toward the bow.

He passed the body of Heath, who had managed to crawl on deck before he died. The remaining member of the crew, Benjamin Matthews, lay bleeding on the deck. Jordan, who had run aft, returned with another axe and finished Matthews off with several strokes to the back on the head. "I might as well be drowned as shot," Stairs thought. He pulled off a hatch cover, threw it over the side, and jumped into the cold Atlantic.

Jordan took aim with a pistol as Stairs crawled onto the hatch cover, but Kelly stopped him from firing. "He'll drown before he reaches shore," the mate assured him. It was a small act of mercy in a bloody afternoon's work that Jordan would live to regret.

Stairs was some four miles offshore, but luck was with him. After clinging to the hatch cover for more than three hours, Stairs was picked up by the American fishing schooner *Eliza*, "weak and almost senseless," by his own account. A hardy man, to say the least, Stairs recovered quickly, described the brutal murders to his rescuers and borrowed a spyglass.

He spotted two schooners on the horizon, but *Eliza*'s captain, Stoddard, refused to change course to see if either was *Three Sisters*. If he deviated from his voyage and had an accident, it would not be covered by insurance, he told Stairs. When Stairs asked to be put ashore at Halifax, Stoddard again refused. The port was rife with press gangs seeking sailors for the British navy in the war against Napoleon. *Eliza* had been stopped at sea earlier in the voyage and had lost its pilot. Stoddard would risk no more of his crew. The schooner docked at its home port of Hingham, Massachusetts, just south of Boston, later in the month, and Stairs reported the piracy. On September 27, Boston port authorities began circulating an account of the crime and descriptions of Jordan, his wife, and Kelly. The three pirates had a two-week head start.

The news did not reach Halifax until October 17. The city's *Royal Gazette* published the Boston circular and a letter Stairs wrote to the owners of *Three Sisters*, Halifax merchants Jonathan and John Tremain, describing his ordeal. Another Halifax newspaper termed it "an act of barbarity" perpetrated by "the most diabolical incendiaries in human shape." A week later Nova Scotia's governor, Sir George Prevost, offered a one hundred pound reward to anyone who could bring "those atrocious villains to that punishment they so justly merit." To sweeten the pot, the Tremains offered a one hundred pound reward, and the insurers kicked in a further one hundred pounds.

The schooner's heading when last seen by Stairs—southward from Cape Canso—was the only lead, but the chances of capture were good. *Three Sisters* was only two days from its destination, Halifax, when commandeered and would have to take on supplies. In early November, the British navy schooner *Cuttle*, sailing into Bay Bulls on the southeastern coast of Newfoundland, overtook a black-hulled schooner, about sixty tons, with a yellow streak along the gunwale. It matched the description of *Three Sisters*. On board were a black-bearded man and a woman with four children under the age of nine—undoubtedly Jordan and his family. *Cuttle*'s captain had the couple and two seamen found on board arrested and put in leg irons. Kelly, the mate, had left the vessel only hours before and remained at large.

Cuttle reached Halifax on November 10. If Jordan was on deck, he would have witnessed a prophetic sight as the schooner passed McNabs Island and entered the harbour—the bodies of six men convicted of mutiny on *HMS Columbine* were hanging in chains on Maugher's Beach. The colony's chief justice, Sampson Salter Blowers, ordered Jordan and his wife to stand trial later in the week. In the meantime, a dispute erupted over how the case would be tried. Under the law of the day, there was no jury in piracy cases. Instead, such cases were heard by a special court consisting of the governor and his council, the judge of vice-admiralty, the colony's secretary and all naval officers of the rank of commander and above. The Jordans faced trial by an unwieldly committee of fifteen.

It was the admiralty judge, Alexander Croke, who turned the procedure into a sideshow. "Haughty, arrogant and vindictive," wrote one historian, "Croke early became the most disliked man in Halifax." In December 1808 he temporarily took over the colony while the governor, Prevost, was directing the British capture of the West Indies island of Martinique and managed to enrage virtually everyone who dealt with him. A year later, Croke was ready to flex his muscles again. He bluntly claimed he should have precedence over the governor in the court of piracies trying Jordan. Crown officials consulted sided with the governor; Croke, his ego bruised, refused to sit on the court at all. Blowers, considered "a hardworking, painstaking judge," took his place.

The two-day trial opened November 16. The prosecutor, Solicitor General James Stewart, called only three witnesses. Stairs described the grisly events of September 13 and denied he had any dispute or quarrel with Jordan before the first shot was fired. Patrick Power and John Pigot, the two seamen arrested with Jordan, testified they were recruited in Newfoundland to man *Three Sisters*. Kelly posed as the schooner's captain, and Jordan said their destination was Ireland.

Both men had their suspicions about the vessel. Its cargo of fish was poorly stowed in the hold and a hatch cover was missing. But Jordan kept them on board with a mixture of lies and threats. The pair also spent much of their time keeping the Jordans apart. Jordan repeatedly threatened to kill his wife, who in turn began hinting to the newcomers that "you know not the mischief [Jordan and Kelly] have done."

Margaret Jordan's lawyer, a prominent Loyalist politician and future Supreme Court judge named Lewis Morris Wilkins,

131

scored some points in his cross-examination. Stairs admitted he was not injured by the blows she inflicted with the boat hook. Pigot agreed Jordan's wife seemed to acting out of "great fear" of her husband.

Then it was Jordan's turn. It was not the first time Jordan faced the death penalty; in 1797 he was sentenced to death by firing squad for his part in an Irish rebellion, but he escaped and was later pardoned. Now, speaking in his own defence, Jordan claimed he was the rightful owner of *Three Sisters* and the Tremains had "surreptitiously" taken the ship from him. The Halifax merchants later published a denial, maintaining that Jordan signed the schooner over to them to settle a debt.

Turning to the events of September 13, Jordan said he had booked passage on the schooner with his family and, after drinking heavily, caught Stairs "taking liberties" with his wife. According to Jordan's account, a fight ensued and Stairs shot at him and missed, killing Heath instead. Jordan said he made it to the deck and armed himself with a handspike. Stairs followed, threw the hatch overboard and jumped over the side. Jordan claimed he tried to get the mate to turn back for Stairs, but Kelly "seemed stupid" and did not want to change course for fear of becoming lost.

Margaret Jordan, in a written statement read to the court by Wilkins, backed up her husband. She said Stairs had indeed taken liberties but Jordan came to her aid. In the confusion, she said, she might have struck Stairs, but only to defend her husband. But the couple had not been able to get their stories straight. Margaret Jordan had Heath being shot on deck, not below. And neither prisoner explained what happened to the second murdered crewman, Matthews.

The court adjourned for thirty minutes before returning a unanimous verdict of guilty against Jordan on charges of piracy, murder and robbery. Asked if he had anything to say before the death sentence was passed, Jordan simply asked if the court had examined his documents outlining his dealings with the Tremains. As for Margaret Jordan, Prevost said the court had considered "some circumstances that appeared to be in her favour" and found her not guilty. Halifax clergymen soon took up a collection to help her and the children return to Ireland.

Jordan was hanged a week later; his body was left to rot on a beach south of the city, in what later became Point Pleasant Park. In a confession published after his death, Jordan said he was destitute and commandeered the ship "in a moment of desperation." While admitting he tried to kill Stairs, he said he meant no harm to come to Heath or Matthews. He also absolved his wife and Kelly of any involvement in the murders.

Kelly was rounded up in Newfoundland and brought back to Halifax in early December for trial. This time a chastened Croke swallowed his pride and took part. After re-hearing testimony about the piracy and new evidence from Margaret Jordan and several character witnesses, the court deliberated for less than an hour and found Kelly guilty.

"His appearance on the trial was that of a simple, timid lad," the *Royal Gazette* reported. Faced with evidence that Kelly had been corrupted by Jordan, the court was inclined to mercy. Prevost imposed the death sentence but told Kelly the court would recommend a pardon. It was later granted. By taking all the blame, Jordan, who ruthlessly dispatched two men to their deaths, helped save one young sailor from sharing his fate.

Chapter 12

The *Saladin* pirates

The masts and sails of the square-rigger gradually emerged from the thick fog as Captain Cunningham's boat drew near. Heavy surf, whipped by a strong onshore wind, pounded the vessel, which was stuck fast on the shore of a small island. Through the fog, Cunningham could see a handful of crewmen struggling to keep their footing as the deck rolled and breakers burst over the stern.

Cunningham, master of a small coastal schooner carrying barrels of pork from Antigonish to Halifax, had taken shelter from the poor weather in Country Harbour on Nova Scotia's Eastern Shore. As his vessel lay at anchor about dawn on May 22, 1844, he was hailed by a group of people on shore. A large ship had run aground on Harbour Island, one of three large islands at the mouth of the harbour. Cunningham and his crew manned a longboat to attempt a rescue.

A line was tossed to the stricken ship. Cunningham, risking his life, tied it around his waist and was hauled through the waves to the ship. One crewman begged Cunningham to take command, saying the others had been drinking and could not handle the vessel. All sails were set, and Cunningham feared the wind would shift, pushing the ship away from shore and into deeper water, where it would undoubtedly sink. He ordered the drunken crew to cut the ropes to let the sails flap freely in the wind.

Cunningham remained on the ship for a day and a half, working feverishly with the crew to salvage the cargo. And what a valuable cargo it was: several tons of copper; thirteen bars of

134

silver, each weighing 150 pounds; a chest filled with gold coins; and a number of letters containing money. In all 18,000 pounds worth of goods were saved from the wreck. But the main cargo, barrels of guano—bird droppings used as fertilizer—was lost. By the time Cunningham left the vessel to the whim of the sea, it was lying on its starboard side, guano washing out of large holes poked in its bottom.

On shore, the authorities were more interested in answers than salvage. Six men were on the ship when it went aground, too few to man such a large vessel. The crew claimed the captain, Alexander McKenzie, had died at sea two months earlier, not long after leaving Valparaiso, Chile, for the British Isles. After that, the mate and two crewmen had fallen from the rigging and were lost overboard.

The story seem plausible, and the crewmen were allowed to leave. But another story would soon emerge, a story of treachery, greed and murder that stands without parallel in Nova Scotia's long history of seafaring. The ship that chance had tossed onto the province's shore had been christened *Saladin*. It was a name that would grow to be synonymous with the word mutiny.

The bloody tale of *Saladin* begins in late 1842, when Captain George Fielding sailed from Liverpool, England, as skipper of the barque *Vitula*, bound for Buenos Aires. The son of a British soldier, Fielding was raised in the Gaspé. By the time he reached middle age, he had a reputation as a scoundrel; an acquaintance once expressed surprise that Fielding had managed to escape the gallows. "A most determined villain," noted one writer, a conclusion that Fielding's actions would bear out.

Finding freight rates low in Argentina, Fielding sailed around the Horn to Valparaiso, but fared no better. Then he hit upon a scheme to turn a fast, if illegal, buck. Heading up the Pacific coast to Peru in July 1843, he tried to smuggle a load of guano. But as *Vitula* tied up, Fielding was greeted by a force of 50 Peruvian soldiers intent on seizing the vessel. Fielding distributed arms to his crew to repulse the boarding party, but the seamen had other plans and fled below deck. Undaunted, Fielding tried to head back to sea. He was cutting the cable with a carving knife when a soldier shot him in the shoulder.

The ship was seized and taken to Callo, a port near the capital of Lima, where Fielding and the crew were thrown in prison. But the crafty Fielding was not to be outdone. Helped by his teenaged son, George, he escaped. Father and son hid for two days on the waterfront before fleeing on a British steamer bound for Chile. Fielding was a desperate man. His ship was gone, confiscated by the Peruvians. His only possessions were a few clothes, his navigation instruments and charts, and a Bible. For months he tried in vain to secure passage to England.

Enter Alexander McKenzie, master of the Newcastle-based *Saladin*, a 550-ton barque easily idenified by its figurehead—a bronzed bust of a Turk complete with turban, earrings and thick moustache. McKenzie had been at sea twenty years and was a sailor's nightmare. Archibald MacMechan, the great Nova Scotia storyteller, described McKenzie as "an old-fashioned, driving, swearing, drinking, capable son of Neptune." Noted another writer: "He ruled his crew with a will of iron, bellowed his commands and frequently hastened action with his feet or fists." McKenzie's temperament won obedience but little admiration: When his back was turned, *Saladin's* eleven crewmen showed their disrespect by calling him Sandy.

For reasons known only to McKenzie, he took pity on his stranded countrymen, agreeing to take Fielding and his son to England for free. But *Saladin* had barely cleared Valparaiso for London when McKenzie began to regret his uncharacteristic kindness. "Frequent differences occurred between Capt. McKenzie and Capt. Fielding; the latter in consequence would often refuse to come to [the] table at meals," noted George Jones, the ship's sailmaker. "When Captain McKenzie came on deck, Fielding several times cursed him and used abusive language." As McKenzie told the mate, Bryerly, "it served him right for giving Fielding a passage free." The two men were probably too much alike to get along. There could only be one captain of *Saladin*, and Fielding was determined it would be him.

After the ship turned north into the Atlantic, Fielding made his move. He convinced four men to join him in a mutiny. Given McKenzie's rough treatment of the crew, it probably took little persuasion. For good measure, Fielding recruited his henchmen with a combination of threats and promises. Join him, he said, and win a share of the valuable cargo. Side with McKenzie and die.

The chosen four were a motley crew. Jones, the first man approached, was a dark-haired Irishman whose countenance, according to one newsman, was "expressive of suspicion and treachery." He had lost a leg in a fall from a spar and walked on a wooden stump. John Hazelton, twenty-eight, spoke with a nasal twang that made listeners think he was from the southern states, but he was believed to be a Nova Scotian. William Travaskiss, short and stout, was a twenty-three-year-old Londoner who went by the alias Johnston. He had joined *Saladin* in Chile, claiming he had been discharged from an American warship. Charles Gustavus Anderson, a Swede who spoke broken English, was the son of a master shipbuilder. Although he was only nineteen, he was Fielding's most willing accomplice. When Fielding made his pitch, Anderson is purported to have replied: "By God, I'll take a knife and cut [McKenzie's] throat. He shall no more strike me away from the helm."

The conspiracy almost failed to get off the ground. Jones tried to warn McKenzie that Fielding was out to kill him, but McKenzie cut him off. "You damned Irishman, I want to hear nothing," he snapped. His fate was sealed. The deed was to be done on the night of April 13—appropriately, a Friday—when Anderson, Johnston and Hazelton were on watch. But Jones put another hitch in Fielding's plans by failing to appear on deck to join the mutineers. The plan was put on hold and the next morning Fielding had some words of wisdom for Jones: "There is no use making a fool of yourself; if you go back your life is no more."

Jones, unable to warn McKenzie or back out, showed up the following night. The mutineers armed themselves with hammers, axes and other tools the ship's carpenter had left in one of the lifeboats. The mate, Bryerly, who was complaining of sickness, was lying on the roof of a cabin. He was quickly dispatched with an axe and his body was thrown overboard without a sound.

McKenzie was next, Fielding decided. He sent Anderson and Hazelton to the captain's cabin, but they aborted their mis-

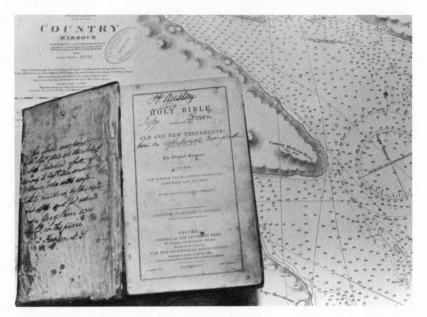

1838 edition of the Bible belonging to the murdered captain of *Saladin*. The inscription reads, in part, "Purchased 10 Sept. 1844 at the Sale of the Ship Saladin's effects ..." (*Chronicle-Herald/Mail-Star* files)

sion, fearing McKenzie's dog would bark and awaken the rest of the crew. Fielding then chose the carpenter as the next victim. As three men waited in ambush around the hatch, they called the carpenter on deck and struck him down. Thinking him dead, they threw him over the side, but the doomed man began to shout after hitting the water.

Fielding saw his chance. "Man overboard!" he shouted. Just as he expected, McKenzie, clutching a Bible he had been reading in his cabin, ran up the companionway and called for the helmsman to come about. As McKenzie emerged on deck, Anderson struck him a glancing blow with an axe. McKenzie grabbed Anderson but was tackled from behind by Jones. As McKenzie wrestled with the two crewmen, he looked up and saw Fielding brandishing an axe. "Damn you, I will give it to you," Fielding yelled, killing McKenzie with two blows. Fielding hauled the body to the side, stuck it a third time for good measure, and threw it overboard.

"The vessel is now our own," Fielding declared, and he invited his followers below for a drink. Fortified with liquor, they went back on deck and discussed how to rid the ship of the remaining five crewmen. It was nearing dawn, so someone called for the morning watch to come on deck. Jem Allen, roused from sleep, walked over to the rail and scanned the ocean. Anderson quietly stole up from behind and knocked him overboard with one swipe of his axe. Thomas Moffat and Sam Collins came up next, and Moffat innocently sat on a spar between Johnston and Hazelton. In a flash his shipmates produced their weapons and Moffat fell to the deck in a pool of blood. At almost the same instant, Anderson murdered Collins with a hammer. Two more bodies were tossed into the sea.

Six men dead, two to go. But, surprisingly, the mutineers balked at the prospect of including the cook, William Carr, and John Galloway, the cabin boy, in their orgy of blood. Perhaps they had had enough killing for one day. When Carr, a middle-aged father of two, came on deck in the morning, he spotted the blood where Moffat had been killed and walked aft to find out what had happened. Gathered around the ship's wheel, he found Fielding, Anderson, Johnston, Jones and Hazelton. At their feet were scattered axes, hammers and other tools, covered with blood.

"What is the matter?" was the best Carr could say in his confusion.

"Come up, we will not harm you," said Fielding. "I am commander of this vessel now. The master and crew have gone away and left us."

Carr looked around and protested that all the lifeboats were in their places. "It is impossible," he stammered. But the truth was slowly sinking in.

"We have finished Sandy," Fielding continued. "We shall have no more cursing and swearing now. We have finished the carpenter, mate, and Jemmy, Moffat and Sam. Will you join us?"

"I suppose if I do not join you, I must go the same road as the rest?" Carr knew the answer. He chose to live.

Galloway, the teenaged son of a Scottish bookseller, was then called. Fielding announced that the captain and the rest of the crew were dead. "I thought they were making sport of me," he recalled, but it was no joke. He too, chose to remain with the living.

Fielding set a new course northward, in the direction of the Gaspé and Newfoundland. His plan was to leave *Saladin* in a secluded cove and return with a new ship to remove the copper, silver bars, and other valuables. Carr was ordered to cook breakfast and Fielding and his cohorts retired to the main cabin and broke into the ship's supply of grog. "They then began to brag which was the best murderer, laughing and jesting with each other," Galloway recalled. On Fielding's instructions they rifled the captain's desk in search of money, then broke into the mail being carried to England. Banknotes intended to cover postage were removed and the letters burned. The dead men's clothing was brought into the cabin and divvied up.

Fielding had two more requests of his willing followers. He ordered all weapons thrown overboard, "because we might get jealous of one another," as Johnston put it. Then Fielding pulled out a Bible. Each man in turn took it in hand and swore to be "loyal and brotherly" to the others. But the strange oath of allegiance would carry little weight among men bound together only by greed and mutual distrust.

The crew quickly discovered there was good reason to be suspicious of their new commander. Even as he swore on the Bible, Fielding was plotting his next move. Still fuming because Carr and Galloway had been spared, he let it be known he wanted them dead before the ship reached land. Two or three days after the murders, Hazelton discovered a set of pistols in the main cabin. The crew confronted Fielding, who denied he had hid them there. But Galloway and Anderson revealed that Fielding had approached each of them with a scheme to kill Johnston, Carr and Jones and increase the survivors' share of the loot.

With that, the men turned on Fielding, binding his hands and feet. A thorough search below deck uncovered a carving knife, gunpowder, ammunition, and jugs of brandy that tasted of poison. Through the night the men argued over what to do. All the while Fielding cursed at them, accusing them of having plotted to kill him. "[He] said we wished to take his life, that we were afraid of him," said Carr.

The next morning Fielding's legs were untied and he was brought on deck. Who decided to impose the death sentence is unclear. Carr and Galloway claimed that the other four—Jones, Johnston, Hazelton and Anderson—compelled them to act. Insisted Carr: "[They] said that Galloway and I should heave Fielding overboard, as we had not committed any other crime, and we should do that to be as bad as them...." Johnston told the same story, but Jones and Hazelton said drowning Fielding was Carr's idea. "Carr said he never would sleep happy till Fielding was overboard," according to Hazelton.

Fielding, realizing the men meant business, begged Galloway to free his hands. The cabin boy refused. Jones and Carr took him to the rail and threw him overboard. Since all feared Fielding's son would turn them in once they reached land, Carr and Galloway seized the boy. He clung desperately to Galloway's sleeve but was shaken off and joined his father in a watery grave.

The remaining six had their hands full manning the ship, and the problem was compounded by frequent drinking. To prevent the ship from being recognized, the figurehead was painted white and a board was nailed over the name on the stern. "We all took an oath never to divulge what had taken place on board the *Saladin*," said Carr. Galloway, the best educated of the lot, assumed the role of navigator, and headed for the Gulf of St. Lawrence. There, the men agreed, they would divide the money, scuttle the ship, and head for shore in a lifeboat. But their plan was dashed on the rocks of Harbour Island.

Saladin's crewmen dispersed after the rescue and headed overland toward Antigonish, where they hoped to find work on other vessels. But questions arose as the authorities began looking through items salvaged from the ship. Some of the clothing was too small for a man, and some charts bore the name of a Capt. George Fielding. The crew was arrested about twenty miles from Country Harbour, and ferried to Halifax in a naval vessel. The six men arrived in late May 1844, in leg irons and under heavy military guard.

They were brought before a judge and, as before, said the captain had died at sea and the other crewmen were lost overboard. Asked about the charts, they explained that Fielding died before the voyage and his personal effects were being taken to relatives in Britain. But documents found on board showed Fielding sold some of his belongings the day before *Saladin* left Chile. As Attorney General James W. Johnston pointed out later, "there were, upon close inspection, local discrepancies, and contradictions in matters of detail" in the stories told by the crewmen. One local newspaper, the *Halifax Journal*, told its readers that "there is great reason to fear that Piracy, if not worse, has been committed."

The crew was locked up until more information could be obtained from Chile, a process that would take months. But inquiries abroad proved unnecessary. On June 8 Carr and Galloway sent for Michael Tobin, a politician who was investigating the wreck as an agent for the insurer, Lloyds of London. Tobin, accompanied by the attorney general and the sheriff, went to the prison and took written statements describing the bloody events on board *Saladin*.

Armed with the new evidence, Tobin visited Hazelton, who refused to co-operate. But over the next few days Johnston, Jones and Anderson signed confessions. Hazelton, approached a second time, followed suit. Charges of murder and piracy were laid against Jones, Johnston, Hazelton and Anderson; Carr and Galloway were to be tried separately for the murders of Fielding and his son.

"Commerce is extending her relations into every portion of the globe, and every sea is whitening with her sails," Attorney General Johnston said, his rich voice echoing through the packed galleries of Halifax's Supreme Court chamber. "It is our duty to throw the protection of the law around those who go down to the sea in ships—it is that alone which can give security to the mariner, and guard the interests of the whole civilized world."

It was a tall order for the court convened in July 1844 to try the first four accused, but Johnston was confident. "One tenth of what these men did would constitute the crime of piracy," he maintained. As he concluded his opening remarks, Johnston admitted the Crown's evidence rested almost entirely on the confessions of those on trial. "Each tried to extenuate and soften his own share in the transaction," he noted, but "there would be found a general agreement running through the whole."

The "general agreement" was that eight men had been murdered, but the confessions raised questions about who killed whom. Anderson, Jones, and Hazelton said Johnston started the ball rolling by murdering the mate; Johnston insisted he was in another part of the ship at the time. Johnston also denied their assertions that he had taken part in the killing of crewman Moffat.

As the attorney general pointed out, each man tried to distance himself from the murders. Anderson freely admitted killing the ship's carpenter and two of the crewmen, but claimed he acted out of fear for his life. "They told me on the night of the mutiny, that if I did not help them, they would kill me." Hazelton said he axed Moffat because "I was afraid if I did not strike, Johnston would strike me." And Jones, whom all agreed had been at the wheel and killed no-one, tried to put the best face on his role in holding McKenzie as Fielding hacked him with an axe. Fielding, Jones said, had threatened "if you don't lay hold of him, I will give you a clout that will kill you."

The confessions of Carr and Galloway were of no help in sorting out the guilty from those compelled to act; both men had been asleep below when the killings occurred. And the others did their best to spread the guilt around. Jones and Hazelton said murdering Fielding was Carr's idea. The same two said Galloway laughed when told McKenzie was dead and expressed regret he had not had a chance to take "a cut at Sandy."

The defence asked few questions and called no evidence. In his closing address, defence lawyer William Young, a short, stout man with a full beard, stressed that Fielding had been the instigator of the crime. Evidence the four had killed out of fear for their own lives "was the only ground of hope for, if not acquittal, at least a recommendation of mercy."

Chief Justice Brenton Halliburton, the presiding judge, rejected outright that thin line of defence. "I can find here no justification, and I regret to add, no ground of excuse for the offence." There had been ample opportunity to warn the others and join them in fighting Fielding's plot. The jury retired for a scant fifteen minutes before declaring all four men guilty. Halliburton took the same hard line when Carr and Galloway stood trial the next day for the murders of Fielding and his son. Nevertheless, both men were acquitted and set free. On Saturday, July 20, the court passed the death sentence on Jones, Anderson, Johnston and Hazelton.

The final scene in the *Saladin* saga was enacted on the morning of July 30 on a hill on the South Common, now the site of Victoria General Hospital. Thousands gathered for the show; one man, William Snyder, walked more than fifty miles from Conquerall Bank, Lunenburg County, to witness the hangings. Soldiers of the Fifty-second Regiment, bayonets fixed, surrounded the scaffold to keep the throng at a respectable distance.

P.H. Lenoir, who was ten years old, recalled her father hitching up the carriage and taking the children. "The big open space was crowded with people. A procession was coming up Tower Road—troops of soldiers, two closed cars, the Sheriff in his gig [a two-wheeled carriage], more soldiers. The four condemned men stepped out of the prison wagon .... They were dressed in black with white shirts. Each man had a coil of rope round his arm, the other end of which was knotted around his neck."

The prisoners, accompanied by clergymen, mounted the gallows; below lay four coffins. The men shook hands and Jones spoke briefly, telling the crowd he was sorry for what he had done and asking for a pardon from God. Lenoir was too far away to hear Jones's words. "White hoods were pulled over their faces," she recalled clearly ninety years later. "The next moment four bodies shot into the air and continued to dangle there. Never have I forgotten the sight."

Mutiny on the *Zero*

When LaHave Island fisherman James Baker boarded the mysterious brigantine on the morning of September 11, 1865, it was under full sail and only a quarter mile from shore. "There was no person to be seen," Baker recalled. "I went on board and saw nothing but a dog." The wheel had been tied off with rope, cabin doors left ajar and, below deck, "everything was upside down and in confusion."

The hull bore signs of an attempted scuttling. On the port side, an axe had been used to chop though the wood near the water line; the other side had been cut with an augur. Neither tool had penetrated the hull, and the hold contained only about two feet of water. Whoever tried to send the vessel to the bottom also wanted its identity to remain a mystery—the name had been painted over in black, leaving only the letter R.

Baker and his companions, eager to claim salvage on the 194-ton ship and its cargo of coal, sailed the brigantine into LaHave harbour on Nova Scotia's South Shore while other fishermen fanned out in search of the crew. One group spotted a small boat beached on nearby LaHave Island. Going ashore, they found three men who said they were from the brigantine *Zero*, which had sprung a leak while carrying coal between Cow Bay, Cape Breton Island, and New York.

The mate, John C. Douglas, did all the talking. The cook, a black man named Henry Dowcey, and the cabin boy, Frank Howard Stockwell, nodded in agreement as Douglas explained that the captain, Colin C. Benson, had been knocked overboard

145

by the boom and lost at sea a few nights earlier. When the five crewmen abandoned *Zero* the previous night, it had six feet of water in the hold and was sinking fast, Douglas claimed. They landed on the island; the remaining crewmen, two Germans named Charles Marlbey and William Lambruert, had run away during the night.

The fishermen reported that *Zero* remained afloat and had little water in its hold. Asked about the attempted scuttling, Douglas offered the dubious suggestion that another vessel had overtaken *Zero*, and its crew had painted out the name and tried to sink the abandoned ship. It was obvious the mate was lying. The fishermen ferried the trio to the mainland, where the authorities would try to find out why.

The mate, cook and cabin boy were brought before a magistrate in Liverpool the following day. All three stuck to the mate's story at the hearing and a subsequent court appearance in Lunenburg. The description of the captain's accidental death was taken at face value and they were released. But suspicions remained and Nova Scotia's attorney general, William A. Henry, ordered Sergeant Lewis Hutt of the Halifax police to investigate. Hutt rounded up Douglas and found Stockwell in Windsor, on the other side of the province. He later tracked down Dowcey, Lambruert and Marlbey in Liverpool and placed them under arrest. While there, Hutt was handed a telegram from Halifax reporting that Douglas and Stockwell had changed their stories. Dowcey, they said, had murdered the captain and cast the body into the sea. The sergeant went to Dowcey's cell with the news. "The mate will get clear because he has turned Queen's evidence," the cook said angrily. It was every man for himself.

Dowcey and the two Germans were shipped to Halifax. After appearing October 10 before a Halifax magistrate in private—an unusual step in those days, later attributed to a desire to prevent evidence from leaking out and prejudicing the trial—Dowcey, Douglas and Lambruert were committed to stand trial for the murder of Benson. "From such hints as transpire from those who have the best means now of knowing facts, we are apt to think that the catalogue of crime has rarely produced a more cruel, brutal murder," reported the *Unionist*, a Halifax newspaper.

The trial opened in Halifax on November 9, 1865, in the newly opened sandstone courthouse on Spring Garden Road. After the presiding judge, Chief Justice William Young, turned down a defence application for the three men to be tried separately, twelve jurors were selected and the Crown opened its case.

Prosecutor Jonathan McCully's star witness was Stockwell, the son of a Springfield, Massachusetts, Baptist minister who had defied his parents and run away to sea. Although only fifteen, he impressed the reporter for the Halifax *Evening Express* as "very intelligent ... everyone who heard him being impressed with the conviction that he was telling the truth."

Stockwell gave a chilling account of Benson's brutal demise. The youth said he had joined *Zero* in New York, as had the cook, Dowcey. Douglas was already on board as mate. When the ship took on coal in Cow Bay, four deckhands were discharged and Marlbey and Lambruert took their place. Other than a minor dispute between the captain and the Germans over wages, it was a routine voyage until Sunday morning, September 10.

Benson turned in about four in the morning, leaving Lambruert at the wheel. Stockwell awoke at dawn and roused the cook, who started a fire in the galley and went forward. Hearing "an unusual noise" coming from the captain's cabin, Stockwell followed but the cook yelled to him to summon Lambruert. Stockwell relieved Lambruert at the wheel. When the German came back on deck, he was wringing his hands in anguish. "The cook has killed the captain," he exclaimed. Relinquishing the wheel, Stockwell headed forward and met Douglas, who was emerging from his cabin. "What's going on?" he asked.

"I don't know," claimed Douglas, whose cabin was located directly across from the captain's. The mate headed into the crew's quarters in the forecastle and Stockwell eventually followed. Inside, Douglas sat on a chest smoking a pipe, surrounded by Dowcey, Marlbey and Lambruert. "Frank, go to the captain's cabin and help the cook," Douglas told Stockwell, who noted tears in the mate's eyes. Stockwell said he would rather jump overboard. Douglas repeated the order to Marlbey and Lambruert. The latter complied.

Stockwell watched as Dowcey and Lambruert carried Benson on deck wrapped in a sheet. One side of his head was bloody and smashed in—the result of four blows Dowcey inflicted with an iron bar as the captain slept—but he was still alive. "Don't, man, and I will go anywhere with you," Benson pleaded as he was tossed into the sea. Stockwell went to the rail. The captain continued to struggle as he floated in the calm sea.

The five crewmen assembled in the forecastle. Douglas and Lambruert were crying, by Stockwell's account, and Dowcey was "half laughing and half crying." Douglas told Dowcey to wash his bloody hands. "God, that's nothing," the cook replied, wiping his hands on his shirt. Dowcey retrieved the captain's papers and handed them to Douglas. "We can't do as we intended," he said after a cursory examination. "There are too many papers, we could not get her to the West Indies or Mexico. She would be missed and a search instituted."

Stockwell testified that Douglas ordered him to burn the papers and the crew divided up the captain's clothes. Dowcey pocketed the captain's gold watch. The crewmen then resolved to head to shore and scuttle the ship. Spotting the beams of two lighthouses in the darkness, they lowered the lifeboat and tried to cut holes in the hull. After the augur broke and the head fell off the axe and was lost overboard, they left the vessel and rowed to shore.

Douglas' lawyer, W.A. Johnston, cross-examined when the trial entered its second day, but managed to establish only that both the mate and the cook gave orders and Douglas seemed afraid of Dowcey "most of the time." Johnston zeroed in on Stockwell's damning statement that Dowcey spoke to Douglas about taking the vessel to the West Indies, "as we intended." "I do not think that he [Douglas] said 'as you intended,'" Stockwell replied, weakly. "He might have said so."

Dowcey was represented by Halifax lawyers W.A.D. Morse and John S.D. Thompson. It was the first major case for Thompson, the future judge, justice minister and prime minister.

He had been admitted to the bar for only three months and turned twenty during the trial. Despite his inexperience, Thompson was called on to present some of the legal arguments on Dowcey's behalf. Given Stockwell's damning testimony, all the lawyers could do was point fingers at Douglas. Questioned by Morse, Stockwell said Douglas and the captain "were not on the best of terms" and the mate had "growled" because he was forced to work on board while the ship was anchored at Cow Bay.

Lambruert's lawyer, Robert Motton, established that Dowcey and Douglas had once sailed together on another vessel. But none of the three lawyers had dented the main thrust of Stockwell's testimony—that Dowcey had badly beaten the captain, possibly in collusion with Douglas, and Lambruert had helped throw him into the sea while he was still alive. Cross-examination "failed to shake him in the slightest degree," in the opinion of one newspaper reporter.

Stockwell's account was backed up by the remaining crewman, Marlbey. What's more, Marlbey testified, he had seen Dowcey and Douglas talking on deck the afternoon before the murder. Dowcey then asked Marlbey to join their plot to throw the captain overboard and sell the ship and cargo. "At first, I thought it was only joking," he told the court through an interpreter. He mentioned the incident to Lambruert, who failed to see the humour and alerted the captain. Benson thanked Lambruert for coming forward, but took no precautions to protect himself. Less than twenty-four hours later, he was dead.

The defence lawyers called no evidence. Morse argued in his summation that there was "no positive proof" Dowcey killed Benson. There was some basis to suspect Douglas, as chief officer, was "the author and instigator of the bloody deed." Johnston countered that Douglas was "doubtless a weak and cowardly man," but he was no murderer. He had gone along with the lie about the captain being knocked overboard by the boom out of fear of Dowcey, but had been the first to recant.

The trial was put over for a third day for the charge to the jury. The chief justice, Young, emphasized the evidence against Dowcey. The case against Douglas was "wholly circumstantial," he warned, but, if the jurors found that the two had formed a plan to murder the captain, it would be a "mockery" not to hold him equally guilty of the crime. The jury retired and were back two hours later with their verdicts. Dowcey and Douglas were found guilty as charged. Lambruert was acquitted.

Lawyers for the convicted men raised legal objections. Dowcey's were dismissed by a full bench of the Supreme Court on November 24, and he was sentenced to hang. Johnston, in a two-pronged attack on the verdict, argued there had not been enough evidence to leave the charge against Douglas to the jury, and the court had the power to set aside the conviction. The mate's sentencing was deferred until the appeal was decided.

On January 3, 1866, the court sustained the conviction by a majority of four to one. Three judges ruled there was evidence of Douglas's guilt that could be left to a jury. Mr. Justice James W. Johnston, a bitter enemy of Young's when the two were in politics, ruled the verdict was wrong, but the court had no power to set it aside. In dissent, Mr. Justice Lewis M. Wilkins said the evidence did not exclude other possible explanations for the mate's actions. He maintained that the court was empowered to quash the erroneous verdict.

The next morning, Douglas appeared for sentencing. Asked if there were any reasons why the death sentence should not be passed, Douglas launched into a lengthy defence of his actions. "I am perfectly innocent of the crime, of which I have been falsely accused," the Halifax *Reporter* quoted him as saying. Douglas said he was sleeping and did not hear Dowcey kill the captain, even though his cabin was close by. After he was awakened by Lambruert and told what had happened, he entered Benson's cabin. Dowcey, "his eyes glaring," was standing over the captain's body. "I was paralyzed at the sight and did not know what to do," Douglas told the court.

Douglas left the cabin and was approached by Marlbey, who asked him to take the vessel to the West Indies. "It flashed on me at once that there was a mutiny," he explained. "I trembled and thought to myself, 'my turn comes next.'" As for Stockwell, the Crown's chief witness, "the young rascal was in the plot."

150

Douglas said Dowcey asked him to help throw the captain's body overboard, but he refused. Dowcey then asked Lambruert, who turned to Douglas to ask permission. "Before I knew what I was about, I answered 'yes,'" Douglas said. "I knew I had done wrong in giving permission. I supposed he was dead all this time. If I had known there was a spark of life in the captain then, I would have died to have saved that spark."

Douglas said he convinced the crewmen the ship was too short-handed to reach the West Indies, and steered a course for shore. He hoped to reach port and turn in the mutineers, but the crew decided to scuttle the ship. Douglas said he went along with the lie about the captain being knocked overboard accidentally because Dowcey had threatened to kill him if he told the truth. "I had to yield to them. I took no command. Throughout, I knew my duty, wanted to do it, but had no power," he told the court, his voice choked with emotion. "I was more like a child than a man—no strength in me."

The chief justice, saying any respite would have to come from the government, sentenced Douglas to hang. Four days later, Dowcey sat in his jail cell and dictated a lengthy statement to his lawyer, Thompson. It was obviously calculated to prevent Douglas from escaping the gallows. "I am truly sorry for what I have done," Dowcey declared, "but I did wrong because I was constantly persuaded to it by the mate."

Dowcey insisted that Douglas had been scheming against Benson all along, and hatched the plot to kill the captain and take the vessel to the West Indies. He had already recruited Stockwell, and asked Dowcey to try to convince one of the Germans to do the killing. "I did not approve of it much," Dowcey said of the plan, but he did as he was told. But he was unable to enlist a killer. The best he could do was to convince Lambruert to help throw the captain overboard after Dowcey stunned him as he slept.

Dowcey provided a horrifying description of what happened after the captain was thrown overboard. The water was dead calm and, as the crewmen sat in the forecastle deciding their next move, they could hear Benson splashing in the water and calling for help. When they emerged on deck he had cleared the stern but he was still struggling to stay afloat. Callously, they stood and watched. "He deserved it. He was nothing but a rogue," Dowcey quoted Douglas as saying.

Dowcey's last-minute allegations had no effect on Douglas's fate. The government, faced with rulings from two of five judges that there was not enough evidence to convict the mate, commuted Douglas's sentence to life in prison at hard labour. "The hand that committed this cruel murder will soon be cold in death," the Halifax *Colonist* noted in reporting government's decision on January 19, "and society will be protected by the life-long imprisonment of his not less guilty accomplice."

About four thousand people signed a petition asking for similar leniency for Dowcey. Hanging only Dowcey in the face of new evidence of Douglas's guilt would "create the impression of a partial failure of justice," a delegation lead by defence lawyers Morse and Thompson argued. The government, although "strongly impressed with the guilt of Douglas," refused to intervene to spare the man who had, by his own admission, inflicted the blows and flung the helpless victim overboard. On January 24, a crowd of about two hundred gathered at the jail yard to watch Dowcey's execution. It was the last public hanging in Halifax.

Who was telling the truth, Dowcey or Douglas? Cowardice alone does not explain Douglas's actions. And it was unlikely Dowcey acted on his own—he could not sail the ship alone, and the others could have easily turned him in. Whatever Douglas's role in the murder of his captain, he never tasted freedom again. *Zero*'s mate died in prison.